STOV

Indian Foe, Indian Friend

Indian Foe, Indian Friend

The Story of William S. Harney

Jules Archer

CROWELL-COLLIER PRESS
COLLIER-MACMILLAN LIMITED / LONDON

Library of Congress Catalog Card Number: 72–93280

The Macmillan Company
866 Third Avenue
New York, New York 10022
Collier-Macmillan Canada Ltd., Toronto, Ontario

Printed in the United States of America

First Printing

To our "fourth son,"
Gary Burdick,
some of whose ancestors were
the first Americans

ACKNOWLEDGMENTS

The author is indebted for the generous coopera-
tion of W. Joynes Macfarlan, Chief, Office of
Information, U. S. Bureau of Indian Affairs; Vic-
tor Gondos, Jr., Chief Archivist, U. S. National
Archives and Record Service, Civil War Branch;
Frederick L. Arnold, Reference Librarian, Prince-
ton University Library; the Director of the Union
Catalogue, Library of Congress; Mary Schutz and
Mrs. Wright of the Mid-Hudson Library system,
Poughkeepsie, N.Y. Acknowledgment is also made
to the Association on American Indian Affairs,
Inc.; the Indian Rights Association; and the State
Historical Society of North Dakota, for source
materials.

Contents

"This Door Has Never Been Open to Indians!"

1

In June 1968, underprivileged American minority groups descended on Washington, D. C., in a "Poor People's Campaign." Setting up crude plywood shelters, they were determined to remain encamped in the nation's capital until Congress recognized their plight and passed legislation to relieve their misery. The five principal groups represented were Negroes, Mexican-Americans, Puerto Ricans, poor whites from Appalachia, and American Indians.

The appearance of Indians in this demonstration startled most Americans viewing the event on television. It was common knowledge that the other groups were being discriminated against under the American system. But *Indians?* Surely any injustices *they* had suffered had long since been made up to them! Most Americans were vague, however, as to exactly what amends had been made to the red men whose country this once was.

A deputation of seventy-five Indians, some in tribal garb and war bonnets, led three hundred impoverished Americans to the stately marble edifice of the United States Supreme Court. Denied admission, the Indians pounded angrily at the great bronze doors.

"We want our rights!" cried Rose Crow Flies High, wife of a Dakota chief. "When will we be given justice?"

"Open these doors!" demanded a Paiute chief from Nevada. "They have *never* been open to Indians. Open them *now!*"

They were not alone in their indignation.

Three months earlier, in March 1968, President Lyndon B. Johnson had sent a stinging message to Congress on American Indian affairs—the first such presidential message in the history of the nation.

"For two centuries," the President said of the American Indian, "he has been an alien in his own land. . . . It has only been 44 years since the United States affirmed the Indian's citizenship. . . . It has been only 22 years since Congress enacted the Indian Claims Act, to acknowledge the nation's debt to the first Americans for their land."

The President spelled out sharply for Congress the tragic plight of American Indians today, after two hundred years of defeat and rule by a society of white conquerors: "Fifty thousand Indian families live in unsanitary, dilapidated dwellings: many in huts, shanties, even abandoned automobiles. The unemployment rate among Indians is nearly 40 per cent—more than ten times the national average. Fifty per cent of Indian schoolchildren—double the national average—drop out before completing high school. Indian literacy rates are among the lowest in the nation; the rates of sickness and poverty are among the highest. Thousands of Indians who have migrated into the cities find themselves untrained for jobs and unprepared for urban life. The average age of death for an American Indian today is 44 years; for all other Americans, it is 65."

He challenged Congress: "No enlightened nation, no responsible government, no progressive people can sit idly by and permit this shocking situation to continue!"

But they have. The original Americans still wait in reservation ghettoes, under the worst possible living conditions, for the justice they have never received under our flag.

A few years ago a young American Indian couple began building a home in a California preserve. A state trooper quickly drove up and told them they could not trespass on public land. The Indian husband insisted that the land belonged to him under a treaty signed by the American government with his tribal forebears. They had been promised the whole freehold, but the promise had been broken. He was simply claiming the tract he would have inherited from his great-grandmother. If anyone was trespassing, he declared, it was not he but the government!

Baffled, the trooper referred the problem back to his superiors. The issue is still bogged down in the courts.

More and more, Indians are seeking redress for injustices done to the red man by the white man in opening up America for European settlement. The federal courts today, now sensitive to the injustices done to the American Negro over the last century, dare be no less fair to another badly mistreated minority—the original owners of America.

President Johnson was not the only national leader to be outraged by the shocking conditions under which most of today's Indians live. Before his assassination, Senator Robert Kennedy headed a new Indian education subcommittee to investigate these conditions on reservations across the country. He planned public hearings in a dozen states, culminating with a national hearing in Washington.

"I am doing my best," he told a group of Indian students in one state, "to get you your civil rights."

"Never mind our civil rights, Senator," one young brave replied wryly. "Just get us back our country!"

The Bureau of Indian Affairs, now part of the United States Department of the Interior, does not attempt to deny the sins of the American government in its dealings with red men.

"In regard to programs seeking to indemnify Indians for past injustices and to rectify wrongs done them," W. Joynes Macfarlan, the bureau's chief of information told this writer, "many programs of the Bureau of Indian Affairs, in a broad sense, are aimed to this end." He pointed out that as of September 1, 1967, the Indian Claims Commission had awarded indemnities of over $241 millions to ninety-two tribes, bands, or groups.

In June of that year, the Federal Claims Court in Washington, D. C., upheld a 1964 commission verdict that the Seminoles and their "cousin" tribe, the Muskogees, had been illegally deprived of their title to thirty-two million acres of Florida land. According to that decision, the Indians were still legally the real owners of 90 percent of Florida today.

The Seminoles' claim went back to 1819 when Spain ceded Florida to the United States. The Spanish had simply ignored the fact that they had no legal claim to the land, which already belonged to its original inhabitants, the Seminoles. During the next twenty-three years, American military forces attacked and killed thousands of Seminoles, then forcibly exiled four thousand survivors to Oklahoma. Only three hundred fifty had escaped into the Everglades, but they and their descendants were obviously still the rightful heirs of modern Florida.

The Federal Claims Court decision of 1967 acknowledged that the Seminoles had never recognized or agreed to either Spanish or American conquest of their lands. This ruling stunned white Floridians. Did the Court actually expect them to return 90 percent of the state back to its Indian owners?

The court, of course, had no such notion in mind.

It simply awarded forty million dollars in government compensation to the Seminoles, a settlement on the basis of $1.25 an acre—the price in 1819. Every penny the United States government had paid in benefits to the Seminoles over the last century was then deducted from the award. But no indemnity was added for the thousands of Seminoles who had been killed defending their land against American troops.

Most Indian wars were started by the white man to exploit the red man or to get him out of the way. When the United States cavalry attacked the Sioux for refusing to be herded onto a reservation, Chief Sitting Bull declared, "We are an island of Indians in a lake of whites. . . . These soldiers want war. All right, we will give it to them."

In popular American folklore and history, Indians have long been portrayed as savages who went on the warpath to make cruel attacks upon brave white pioneers, cowboys, and troops. If Indians had written the textbooks, television, and movie westerns, they might with more justification have depicted white European invaders seizing the land of native Americans, killing those who resisted, and imprisoning those who surrendered in concentration camps known as reservations.

But the cowboys-and-Indians version of American history helped camouflage what anthropologists would describe as a campaign of genocide against the red man in America. The stereotypes of the heroic western settler and the villainous redskin were myths carefully fostered all through the eighteenth, nineteenth, and twentieth centuries. They made it possible to obscure the image of the Indian as a human being, deserving of sympathy and justice, while unscrupulous white businessmen grew rich plundering his furs, his buffalo herds, and his lands.

White children in white schools are taught principally a white version of the origins of their country. They learn that Columbus "discovered" America and that the Pilgrims "settled" it. But Columbus discovered America only for *Europeans*. The Indians didn't need anyone to discover it for them; they were already here. And the Pilgrims didn't settle it, as much as confiscate it from the red man.

Courageous Roger Williams, the founder of Rhode Island, was thrown out of the Massachusetts Bay Colony for insisting on an embarrassing truth—that the Pilgrims were intruders illegally *trespassing* on Indian-owned lands. He was considered the equivalent of a communist for insisting that the least they could do would be to buy the lands honestly.

In short, the true discoverers and settlers of America were the Indians, who had lived here for centuries before the first white man of Europe set foot on the red man's soil.

It is important for tomorrow's citizens to know the truth about the persistent injustices the red man has suffered at the hands of the white man in our country. It is important to understand what drove Rose Crow Flies High, at the head of the Indian delegation of the Poor People's March, to pound at the great doors of the United States Supreme Court and to cry out in anguish to all Americans, "When will we be given justice?"

Within a decade young Americans under twenty-five will constitute a majority of the population. It is to this new generation that the Indian appeal for justice will be addressed. As voters and legislators, they will have to decide what and how much shall be done to make amends to the red man. Amends for leaving him in abject misery while we enjoy unlimited freedom, opportunity, and prosperity in the great land our forefathers stole from his forefathers.

This book will help them understand how it happened.

The complete story of how the Indians lost America would take a hundred volumes to relate. Instead, *Red Man, White Man* attempts to reflect that tragic story through the dramatic prism of one man's life. Lieutenant General William Selby Harney (1800–1876) was one of the most remarkable unsung heroes of American history, and an ideal choice as a camera of his times.

The story of Harney's career tragically reveals how the American government, time after time, bribed Indian tribes off the warpath with peace treaties that the government had no intention of keeping, and which it did not keep. Almost alone among influential Americans of his day, Harney angrily fought this cynical policy of betrayal.

The Indians recognized him not only as a courageous foe in battle, but also as a genuine peacemaker and friend. He, as well as they, was embittered by the refusal of the government he respected, served, and trusted to live up to its pledges to the tribes. As a final irony, powerful enemies finally forced his retirement at a time his country most needed his influence with the Indian nations of America.

"The removal of General Harney," President Abraham Lincoln ruefully admitted afterward, "was one of the greatest mistakes of my administration!"

Young Man with Sword

William Selby Harney was born at Haysborough, Tennessee, not far from Nashville, on August 22, 1800. He was a turn-of-the-century child whose birthdays dated the significant events of the first three-quarters of the nineteenth century.

The United States of his birth had only 5,300,000 persons, exclusive of Indians, occupying only the territory east of the Mississippi and north of Florida. Tennessee, still part of the American frontier, had been a state only four years.

The Cumberland River wilderness that surrounded young Bill Harney's home was thick with river pirates as well as Indian tribes hostile toward settlers who had pushed southwest at the end of the Revolutionary War. The settlers of Haysborough built a picket fence enclosure into which they retreated whenever it was necessary to fight off Indian sieges.

Young Bill grew up with the sound of roaring muskets and whistling arrows in his ears. It was hardly surprising that as a teen-ager he automatically regarded Indians as hostiles to be fought—"them" as against "us."

Cool courage ran in his veins. His father, Thomas, a Marylander of English descent, had been promoted to the rank of major for bravery in the Revolutionary War. During the Battle for Princeton, Major Harney had been in charge of forces held up by a broad, deep river with the British camped on the other side. That night he and a junior officer swam silently across the river, then swam back with enemy boats in tow. The result had been the capture of the sleeping British.

Bill Harney's mother was a spirited, courageous Irishwoman named Margaret Hudson Harney. During one Indian attack when the settlers fled inside the picket fence, the woman entrusted with making bullets was so scared she spilled more lead than went into the molds. Margaret Harney took over the job, coolly ignoring the fighting raging around her as she turned out the needed ammunition swiftly and efficiently.

On another occasion she had discovered her son James, the third of her eight children, in a brawl with one of the unsavory characters who infested the wilderness around Haysborough. She did not interfere until the thug suddenly pulled a bowie knife out of his shirt and slashed James's hand. Then she sprang at him, a towering figure of wrath, denouncing him as a coward and demanding that he give her his knife.

He was so flabbergasted that he surrendered it.

Bill Harney was the youngest of her eight children. His oldest brothers and sisters were, in order of birth, Benjamin, John, James, Robert, Eliza, Margaret, and Thomas.

The two oldest were destined to become physicians. Benjamin served as an Army surgeon in the Indian and Mexican wars.

During young Bill Harney's early years, travel and communication between Tennessee and the rest of the United States were painfully slow, difficult, and perilous. Railroad, telegraph, and steamboat lay years in the future. Each pioneering community was left to its own resources for protection.

Indian hostility grew sharper as more and more settlements intruded into their hunting grounds. Their resentment was scarcely lessened in 1804 when the government initiated a systematic program of forced removal of tribes from their homes east of the Mississippi. This policy developed under President Thomas Jefferson, who had set aside part of the Louisiana Purchase wilderness for an Indian territory.

A distinguished liberal in most respects, Jefferson inexplicably believed in the "self-evident" right of the white man to displace the red man. If necessary, he had repeatedly told George Washington, the Indians should be given a "thorough drubbing," after which "liberal and repeated presents" could then keep the Indian nations pacified.

A typical patriot of his day, Jefferson saw nothing immoral in the concept of kicking the Indians out of their homelands, as long as the government eased its conscience by giving them more distant—if poorer and less desirable —hunting and fishing lands in exchange.

As a young teen-ager it was perfectly understandable that Bill Harney took for his heroes military men who had distinguished themselves fighting the red men he knew only as a dangerous threat to his family and community.

One was General William Henry Harrison, the hero of a battle against Tecumseh's Indian settlement at Tippecanoe, south of what is now Canton, Ohio. Another was General Andrew Jackson, a good friend of his father's, who defeated the Creek Indians in Alabama and won the belated Battle of New Orleans against the British.

The early nineteenth century was an intensely patriotic period of American history. It was during the bombardment of Fort McHenry in the War of 1812 that Francis Scott Key composed the "Star Spangled Banner." Young Bill Harney's idols also included Navy heroes like Captain Oliver Perry, who defeated the British on Lake Erie, and Commodore Stephen Decatur, who ended the blackmail of United States shipping by Barbary pirates.

He could not make up his mind whether he wanted to be another landlocked Harrison or Jackson, or another seatossed Perry or Decatur. Margaret Harney, an ardent admirer of America's naval heroes, had her heart set on having at least one of her sons follow a career at sea.

When Bill was fourteen, his parents sent him to a boys' private academy in Haysborough headed by a Professor Craighead. While he was studying there, the Harneys were visited by an old friend named Jennison, a retired naval captain from Boston. Bill's mother persuaded Jennison to give Bill after-school lessons in navigation. And he prepared to become a sailor.

When he was seventeen, he was allowed to take a vacation visiting his older brother, Dr. Benjamin F. Harney, who was then stationed at Baton Rouge, Louisiana, as an Army surgeon. He journeyed south along the Natchez

Trace, protected from Indian attack by an 1801 treaty with the Chickasaws and Choctaws. The trip nevertheless thrilled him. He had never before been so far away from home all by himself.

While he was staying with his brother Ben, Indian warfare suddenly broke out in adjacent Florida. It began when Georgia backwoodsmen attacked Indians just above the Florida border, and the red men struck back. Secretary of War John Calhoun ordered General Andrew Jackson to "adopt the necessary measures to terminate the conflict." Bill was wide-eyed with envy when his brother received orders to join Jackson's headquarters at Pensacola.

Before leaving, Ben introduced him to General Thomas Jesup, commanding officer of the Baton Rouge base. Jesup was impressed by the seventeen-year-old youth's patriotic zeal, soldierly bearing, and dynamic personality. Learning that Bill was planning a Navy career, the general offered persuasive arguments to change his mind and succeeded.

Three weeks later, he summoned Bill Harney to his office and handed him a commission as Second Lieutenant in the United States First Infantry. Dated February 13, 1818, it was signed by President James Monroe. So at the raw age of seventeen, Bill Harney became an officer of the United States Army.

He felt breathless with pride in his new uniform, sword hilt glistening in the Louisiana sun, brass-barreled Pond flintlock pistol on his other hip. He could scarcely wait for his first assignment which, ironically, turned out to involve more seamanship than soldiering.

He was sent to the Louisiana coast at the mouth of the Mississippi with a regiment ordered to chase pirates in

Atchafalaya Bay. Most were Jean Lafitte's men, who robbed Spanish vessels and smuggled their booty into the United States. They were directed by Lafitte from his headquarters at Galveston, then part of Mexico. The famous pirate was brazen in his operations, feeling he had a protector in Jackson, who had given him a pardon because of Lafitte's services against the British during the Battle of New Orleans.

Harney was determined to excel in his first assignment, and he soon held the regiment's record for pirate ships and booty captured. Cool and courageous to the point of recklessness, he quickly won the confidence of his men.

On one search mission in his little harbor craft, he overhauled a vessel whose papers were not in order. While he inspected the ship's register, its captain told the first mate in Spanish to get their men ready to attack and kill the boarding American soldiers. Harney, who had learned just enough Spanish to understand, moved swiftly.

Seizing the captain, he hurled him down the hatchway. His men swiftly pinioned the pirate crew at gunpoint. A search of the vessel revealed that it was ballasted by hollow iron bars filled with smuggled quicksilver. Taking the ship in tow, they made weigh for New Orleans.

A tropical hurricane swept up suddenly over the bay. Torn loose from their prize, they were carried away almost into the Gulf. Afterward as they sailed home, some of Harney's men became delirious with thirst under the blazing summer sun. Their water was gone, and the storm had filled the bayous with brackish water.

After pulling into several inlets, Harney finally located some fresh water in a hollow cypress log. His jubilation was dampened by the discovery that it was filled with wriggling larvae. Undaunted, he took off his shirt and strained the water through it several times until his men could drink it without revulsion.

His hopes of joining Ben at Jackson's headquarters in Pensacola were dashed by a February treaty with Spain ceding the territory of Florida to the United States. In January 1819, relieved of pirate-chasing duty, he was transferred to Fort Warren in Boston for six months of re-cruiting duty under a major named Brooks. Here Harney first manifested how stubborn he could be when he disa-greed with an order.

Each time Major Brooks left the post, young Harney, as next in rank at the tiny garrison, automatically assumed command in his absence. Some grizzled noncoms protested against having to take orders from "a boy playing sojer."

"You mustn't do it again," Major Brooks ordered.

"I'll continue to take command," the young lieutenant replied coolly, "whenever you leave the post, Major."

The next time he did it, Brooks furiously brought charges of insubordination against him. But a court-martial exonerated young Harney, finding that his behavior was in strict accordance with Army regulations. It was the first, but far from the last, run-in he would have with superior officers.

He rejoined his regiment at Baton Rouge in late June. When Lafitte's pirates attacked an American merchant ship in the Gulf area, Harney was ordered to find their lairs and destroy them. His search-and-destroy missions suc-ceeded so well that he forced Lafitte to move the pirates' base of operations to the Spanish Main.

In July 1821, to his great delight, he was ordered to Pensacola to serve as commander of the guard for General Andrew Jackson. He knew that the honor was more than just recognition for his successes against Lafitte. His brother Ben had been transferred to another post, but Bill Harney was sure Ben had probably put a word in for him with Jackson. The general was, in addition, a good friend of his father's and a Cumberland Valley neighbor of the Harney family.

Jackson had recently been commissioned governor of Florida by President James Monroe. Nine years earlier during the War of 1812, Indian tribes in Georgia and Alabama had fought a guerrilla war on England's side. Jackson had driven Creek Indians back into the forests and glades of Spanish Florida.

The Florida Indians began to be known as Seminoles, presumably after the Indian word for "runaways." But Seminole really meant "wild people"—Indians who preferred their own way of life to that of the white man. They had been joined in the cypress swamps by runaway Negro slaves and other Creeks from Georgia. Some slaves became slaves of the Seminoles, who treated them kindly. Others were given complete hospitality as fellow refugees from the white man and were permitted to intermarry into the Seminole tribes.

Angry slaveowners from Georgia had pursued fugitive slaves into Florida, but were fought off by the Seminoles as bandits and foreign invaders. President Monroe had authorized Jackson to pursue and subdue the tribes, so in 1814 the general had invaded the territory of Florida.

The Indians were "taught a lesson" by raids on their

villages that killed three hundred Seminole men, women, and children, wounding hundreds more. They fled deep into the swamps. The choice lands they left behind were quickly settled by white men moving across the Florida border behind the protecting shield of Jackson's troops.

Jackson made the rape of Florida official by pressing Spain—which could not defend it, anyhow—to sell it to the United States for five million dollars. Spain had inserted a face-saving clause in the treaty requiring the American government to respect the rights of Florida's Indians and to deal with them justly. Jackson shrugged and signed.

Within a matter of hours the slave-catchers were given a free hand. Capturing hundreds of runaway slaves, they also seized the children of Indian-Negro marriages, and even pure-blooded Indians, to sell on the slave marts of Georgia.

When Lieutenant Bill Harney arrived in Pensacola to take his place as one of Jackson's aides-de-camp, the First Seminole War was drawing to a close. Jackson greeted him warmly, introducing him to General Edmund P. Gaines as "one of our brighter young officers." During his months on Jackson's staff, Harney was treated as a protégé of the fifty-four-year-old governor. He listened with awe to every word spoken by the military hero of his boyhood.

"The one word that must not be in your vocabulary is retreat," Jackson instructed him. "Determine to die rather than give way in the face of the enemy. It is not only a matter of personal pride. It is the duty a soldier owes to his country. With Indians, especially, never show fear or make any concessions. The red man respects only courage."

In Jackson's view, it was unwise to seek treaties with the Indians. He believed in using force against them until *they* asked for peace terms. He told Harney about Chief Weatherford, a Creek responsible for a massacre at Fort Mims in Georgia.

"I paid the Creeks back for that, I can tell you," he declared. "As Davy Crockett said, 'We shot them like dogs.' I tried to get my hands on Weatherford, but he was an eel. Once he escaped by leaping his horse off a steep bluff into the river below."

When Jackson had finally compelled the Creeks to sue for peace, he had refused to parley until they first surrendered Weatherford for punishment. A few days later a tall, light-skinned Indian, naked to the waist, had walked alone into the American general's tent. To Jackson's astonishment, he identified himself as Chief Weatherford. Jackson had flared, "How *dare* you show yourself at my tent, after having murdered the women and children at Fort Mims!"

"I have come to give myself up," Weatherford had replied. "I am in your power. Do with me as you please. If I had any warriors left I would still fight you, but I cannot call the dead to life. I now ask for peace for my people, not for myself. Your people have destroyed my nation. Our best warriors are slain, our cattle and grain destroyed, and our women and children are destitute. You are a brave man—I rely on your generosity. Whatever your terms, it would be madness in us to oppose them. I hope you will exact no terms for a conquered people but such as they should accept."

Impressed with his dignity and courage, Jackson had offered him a cup of brandy and a proposal. He would spare Weatherford and also provide food for the starving Creek women and children, he promised, if the chief would agree to enforce peace among his people. They shook hands on it.

But Jackson had sought to impose crushing terms on the defeated Creeks—"reimbursement" for his military campaign, which he set at twenty-three million acres, or half the Creek territory in what is now most of Alabama and a portion of Georgia. It had not mattered to him that much of this land belonged to Creeks who had not even fought against him, and some of it to Creeks who had even helped him against Weatherford. All Creek chiefs had been forced to sign the treaty.

Thousands of Creeks fled from Georgia into Florida rather than submit. The series of agonizing Seminole wars that followed had its origins in Jackson's avarice. To the white America of his time, however, he was a double hero —victor over the British at New Orleans and an expansionist who had extended the borders of the United States at the expense of the "savages."

A great cry arose that he run for President. So in November 1821, he turned the command of Florida over to General Gaines, who inherited Harney as an aide.

"With my dysentery, cough and lung inflammation," Jackson told them, "I am scarcely fit to be considered for the presidency. But if my country needs me, I must submit."

The young aide-de-camp was eager to pit his military skill, so far tested only in chasing pirates, against Indians. Gaines gave him permission to lead some mopping-up patrols into the Everglades. At first his troops could scarcely keep up with his eager plunge through the swamps. But the Seminoles seemed to have vanished completely. As days passed without any skirmishes, Harney grew bored.

Then he came across a deserted village in which he found orphaned Indian children starving in the ashes of burned-out cypress chickees. He began passing the smoldering remains of one Seminole village after another. The whole area had the smell and look of a vast grave, as though a dreadful pestilence had swept through it.

His eagerness for battle with the Indians gradually began to cool, and his men found him silent and reflective. In the headquarters at Pensacola, the "redskins" being exterminated by Jackson's forces had seemed little more than animal-like nuisances who had to be hunted down and destroyed.

But here in the ruins of their homes they ceased to appear to him as "Injuns"—they were, he realized, families of men, women, and children. Perhaps if he himself had been born this far south, he, too, might have been a Seminole fighting desperately against white invaders of his village.

He found himself wondering about General Jackson's insistence that Indian treaties were futile. Were the red men really so barbaric that there was no way of dealing with them except to burn their villages and wipe them out?

Returning to Pensacola, he prudently said nothing to General Gaines about his doubts over the government's Indian policy, but continued to struggle with them in private. He did not question the need—or inevitability—of the white man's expansion into Indian lands. He accepted the explanation General Jackson had once given him.

"No matter where the white man's borders are," the general had said, "there will always be hostile Indians on the edge of those borders raiding him. To protect American settlers, it will always be necessary to occupy and pacify the zones outside them. That process, repeated time and again, will inevitably dispose of the Indian problem in battle and raise our flag over all of what now are Indian lands."

What disturbed young Harney, however, was Jackson's assumption that white expansion could not be achieved without total extermination of the Indians. It was one thing to kill red warriors in battle, but another to slaughter Indian women, children, and old men at the same time.

A seditious notion began to take shape in his mind. Why *couldn't* the white man and the red man share America peacefully by treaty? Perhaps, he reflected, if the Army did not do the kind of thing he saw around him in the Everglades, the red man would be more willing to reach and abide by an amicable understanding that would end all Indian wars.

That idea was to become the goal of his life.

Man-who-runs-
like-the-Deer

3

With the First Seminole War seemingly at an end, Harney returned to routine assignments in Louisiana and Mississippi. A respiratory ailment brought on by bivouacking in damp bayous and swamps forced him to apply for sick leave. He spent it back home in Tennessee with his family, then won a brief transfer to the more healthful dry climate of New Hampshire at Fort Constitution. In August 1824, he rejoined the First Infantry at Jefferson Barracks in St. Louis, Missouri, then a frontier town of only five thousand people.

Missouri had been in the Union only four years, and Jefferson Barracks was built as a military outpost to protect Missourians from hostile Indians in the wilderness to the west and northwest. Powerful tribes—the Crows, Mandans, Sioux, and Gros-Ventres—controlled both sides of the Missouri River, down which pirogues, flatboats, and keelboats traveled at their own risk.

French settlements in this area of the Louisiana Purchase had had no difficulty with these tribes. Governing mildly with tact, fairness, and polite respect for Indian dignity, the French were enormously successful both in trading with and living at peace with the red man. They also pleased the Indians by adapting themselves to tribal habits and customs in their mutual dealings. And being moderate wine-drinkers, the French did not—as other white men did —attempt to corrupt and befuddle Indians by giving them "firewater."

These policies made a great deal of sense to the young Army lieutenant. He began to wonder how he might adapt them to influence operations of the First Infantry.

But the new Bureau of Indian Affairs, created in 1824 within the War Department by Monroe, made it clear that the French notion of Indian policy was utterly unacceptable to the American government. The bureau, which was soon called the Indian Service, was dedicated to using the Army to push the red man farther and farther west.

While the First Infantry was in garrison, Harney found the Indian problem far less absorbing than the company of the beautiful French girls of St. Louis. They in turn found the twenty-four-year-old American lieutenant, now extraordinarily handsome in a virile, trim black beard, a delightful companion. He was in great demand at the city's social affairs.

What bothered him most about regimental duty was its purpose—to make the region safe for English-speaking traders who fast-talked Indians out of valuable furs and skins in great demand back east, in exchange for rum and whiskey, rusty guns, faulty ammunition, shoddy utensils, and cheap ornaments. Their unscrupulous practices were provoking a steadily growing number of Indian outbreaks.

Harney wondered uneasily what could be done to ease the rising tension.

Both in the field and in garrison, foot-racing was a popular soldier sport of the day, just as it was among Indian tribes. Harney, tall, spare and muscular, enjoyed pitting his long stride and great powers of endurance against challengers. There was enthusiastic wagering, from coins among the troops to as much as ten thousand dollars among wealthy civilian spectators who came to Jefferson Barracks to watch.

Winning every race he entered, Harney was soon acknowledged to be the First Infantry's champion runner. That gave him the idea he had been looking for.

Why not hold challenge races with the Indians?

He proposed the idea to the First Infantry's commanding officer, pointing out the French example of avoiding Indian wars by pursuing a good neighbor policy. General Henry Atkinson pondered. If the infantry emerged victorious from such a match, they would certainly win increased Indian respect. On the other hand, he worried, if they lost . . .

Harney promised that he would not lose. And so Jefferson Barracks issued invitations to the long-haired Crows to match their best runners against Lieutenant Bill Harney. The Indians accepted the challenge at once. The races took place just outside the log walls of the fort.

Running with the long strides that made him seem to leap through the air, Harney out-paced his startled Crow competitors, one after the other, to the delight of his fellow soldiers. The impressed Crows awarded him an Indian name—Man-who-runs-like-the-Deer. His reputation spread swiftly among the tribes of the upper Missouri. General Atkinson warmly congratulated him on winning prestige for the Army in these early American Olympics.

But Harney's races with the Indians could not prevent mounting indignation over the larcenous operations of the American Fur Company. John Jacob Astor's traders would get the Indians drunk, cheat, and rob them of furs and skins, then sell them tobacco at $18 a pound and whiskey at $50 a gallon. The Winnebagoes, Sioux, Sauks (Sacs), and Foxes not only lost all of their pelts this way, but also ended up deeply in debt to the company. Astor would then seize their lands in payment.

The government also operated Indian trading posts. These offered decent merchandise in exchange for furs and land, but were not allowed to sell liquor or firearms. Astor's agents peddled both and also persuaded the Indians that the better goods sold at the federal trading posts were shoddy.

Whenever disillusioned Indians sought to bring Astor's agents to justice, they discovered that the white man's courts had made Indian testimony "illegal." This law permitted the white man to debauch, deceive, swindle, and murder the red man without fear of Indians testifying against him in court. Not surprisingly, infuriated red men began killing Astor's agents, and one hundred and fifty of these traders lost their lives.

Indian Bureau agents operating the government trading posts sought to have Astor's unscrupulous traders barred from the Indian Territory. Indian Agent G. C. Sibley angrily warned white settlers, "Your property will be sacrificed; your families murdered, and your farms desolated;

but these men insist upon their rights, and the fur trade must be left open to them. . . . What is the bleeding scalp of an infant, compared with the rich fur of a beaver skin?"

Some Indian agents resented Astor's men primarily because they were working rackets of their own. They not only swindled the Indians to line their own pockets, but also swapped merchandise for Indian land at a price of two cents an acre. Bribes changed hands in Washington and in state legislatures, and these mineral-rich "public lands" ended up in private hands.

Not a man to tolerate competition in his swindling operations, John Jacob Astor succeeded in having the government trading posts abolished, giving the American Fur Company an absolute monopoly of the fur trade in the west.

Provoked by these corrupt practices of the white man, the Sioux, Auricheras, Crows, Gros Ventres, Sauks, and Foxes began gathering for war councils at Two Thousand Mile Creek. Missouri braced for serious trouble.

"These white men are not as the French," one Sioux chieftain told his assembled fellow chiefs. "They are not the Canadian trappers, the traders from St. Louis, and the Jesuit missionaries we have known. They are a different breed who come not as friends but as plunderers. If we do not unite and take to the warpath, they will weaken us with their firewater, rob our goods and lands, and end destroying us."

Hearing of the war councils, General Atkinson sped a warning to Washington. A regiment of the First Infantry was ordered to start north for Two Thousand Mile Creek to do everything possible to prevent a war alliance of the tribes, and to persuade the Indians to sign a peace treaty.

Atkinson left at once, taking with him a flash-tempered aide, Major Benjamin O'Fallon, and Lieutenant Bill Harney in command of the troops. Atkinson was hopeful that Harney's prestige among the tribes of the upper Missouri would be helpful in winning their friendship. He told Harney as much.

"You don't really expect them to set aside their grievances, General," the young lieutenant asked in surprise, "just because they admire my ability as a runner?"

"Naturally not. But your being there will help create the relaxed atmosphere we'll need for our councils."

Harney led their expedition of about five hundred soldiers in keelboats loaded with ammunition and supplies up the Missouri. It was slow, backbreaking work against the swift-flowing current. Soldiers naked to the waist worked in teams, putting their shoulders to poles pressed sternward into the river bottom to propel the keelboats upstream.

Often the current was so strong they had to hug the shore and wind bow cables around trees. Then all hands would haul back on the cables to force the boats forward inches at a time. Treacherous sandbars compelled them to cross and recross the river to opposite banks. Sometimes a lead boat would run aground on a bar, stopping with a swash and a grind until the men splashed into the river to lighten her and to force her free by sheer brute strength.

After a hard day's work they would be rewarded with a "fillee" or ration of whiskey, accompanied by a miserable supper of half-burned meat and half-baked bread prepared on the shore where they camped overnight. In this strenuous fashion, they struggled upriver for eight or nine weeks.

By the time they reached Old Council Bluffs, fifteen miles above the tiny trading post of Omaha on the west bank of the Missouri, winter was setting in. The men were ill, exhausted, and short-tempered. The expedition made its winter camp at a site afterward known as Fort Atkinson.

No man on the journey survived its hardships in as fine a shape as William Harney, whose hard muscles testified to his enjoyment of working beside his men.

At this period of his life, according to his friend Jefferson Davis, he was "physically, the finest specimen of a man I ever saw. Tall, straight, muscular, broad-chested and gaunt-waisted, he . . . would run faster than a white man, further than an Indian." He was "also a bold horseman, fond of the chase, a good boatman, and skilful in the use of the spear as a fisherman." Davis attributed Harney's prowess as an outdoorsman to avoidance of common weaknesses of garrison life on the frontier—drinking and sacrificing sleep to spend half the night gambling by campfire or lantern.

In the early spring, the regiment moved up to Two Thousand Mile Creek, leaving behind a detachment to build a fort at Council Bluffs. They would need it if the parley failed. General Atkinson sent scouts ahead with word that he wished to meet with the tribal chiefs who had been holding councils of war. The regiment was given safe conduct to a Mandan village of circular earth lodges, not far from Prairie du Chien. They reached this rendezvous on April 18, 1825.

Leaving their troops, except for a small escort, outside the palisade of stakes enclosing the village, Atkinson, O'Fallon, and Harney were guided to the Mandan chief's lodge. It was large enough to have horses stabled at one side. Buffalo dance headdresses, shields, spears, and combination bow-lances hung from the treetrunk poles that braced the roof. In the sunlight pouring through the smoke hole, Harney saw a dozen painted chiefs, arrayed in full war regalia, waiting for them in silence.

After an exchange of formal greetings, the Indians seated themselves crosslegged in a semicircle, their faces stolid and impassive. Harney was impressed with the great dignity of their bearing, matching in pride the erect carriage of the American officers. The council began.

One chief after the other rose to express curtly the complaints of his tribe against the United States government. All the tribes present, warned the chief of the Auricheras, had voted to take to the warpath together if the Great White Father in Washington did not promise to end these practices.

"Before we can address ourselves to those complaints," replied General Atkinson, "there is a demand from the Great White Father that must first be met. The British have complained that the chief of the Foxes is holding some prisoners captured from a tribe in the British possessions. These men are British subjects, and the British Minister has asked our Government to have them restored. This must be agreed to, my friends and brothers, before we can talk further."

The chief of the Foxes rose, a grim figure in a neck scarf, loincloth, and roach headdress. "The British prisoners shall be freed," he said coldly, "but only after they are ransomed and paid for."

Major O'Fallon, whose nerves were raw from the ordeal of the long journey up the Missouri, reacted to the Fox chief's defiance with hysteria. Neither General Atkinson nor Harney had realized that he was so close to the breaking point. He sprang at the Indian leader screaming insults.

"You'll give those prisoners back without any ransom at all, you dirty red heathen!" he yelled. Before either Harney or Atkinson could stop him, he drew his horse-pistol and struck the Fox chief with the barrel. The Indian staggered under the blow, but did not change expression. O'Fallon smashed the gun against his face a second time.

Whirling, he swung the weapon at two of the seated chiefs, inflicting bloody wounds. All the chiefs quickly reached for the rifles beside them. For a moment there was stunned silence as each man in the lodge, red and white alike, tried to grasp the reality of what had happened. Only a miracle now could prevent the extermination of the troops at the Mandan village, and touch off a new full-scale Indian war.

Harney did not wait for orders from General Atkinson.

Springing from his seated position on the peace blanket, he lunged up at the berserk Army major. His powerful swing caught O'Fallon on the side of the jaw and sent him flying. Leaping on top of the enraged officer, he twisted the gun out of his hands and pinned his wrists to earth.

At Atkinson's crisp order, three soldiers seized O'Fallon and hustled him off to the troop encampment outside the Mandan village. The lodge was ominously still.

Blood poured down the faces of the three Indian chiefs O'Fallon had attacked. Their fellow chiefs had risen, mouths grim and rifles ready. Warriors attracted by the commotion were running toward the council house by the hundreds. If a showdown was at hand, Harney estimated quickly, he and his troops were outnumbered by at least ten to one.

Brushing the dust from his uniform, and moving slowly to give himself time to think, Harney approached the sullen semicircle of armed chiefs. When he addressed them, his voice was quiet and conciliatory.

"The action of our brother was the behavior of a madman," he apologized. "He has not been sleeping well. His mind was as the mind of one unsettled by firewater. We greatly regret the wounds he has caused, and ask the forgiveness of our red brothers." He held out his hand to the chief of the Foxes. "Will you give me a sign of understanding and friendship?"

The injured warrior stared at him grimly, keeping his arms folded. "There will be no return of the British prisoners, without ransom," he said icily. "If this does not satisfy our white brothers, then let there be no peace treaty."

Harney glanced at Atkinson. The general nodded.

"Very well. Give the order to release the prisoners, and you have my word for it."

The Fox chief looked unimpressed. But the head of the Crow nation said, "He who speaks is Man-who-runs-like-the-Deer."

The Fox chief hesitated, then slowly took Harney's hand.

Order was restored and the negotiations continued with

Harney substituting for O'Fallon as General Atkinson's aide. A ransom for the British prisoners was agreed upon, and the white officers agreed to press the Indian chiefs' grievances upon the Great White Father. On those terms, General Atkinson signed a peace treaty for the American government, with each chief signing for his own Indian nation.

The chief of the Mandans, an impressive warrior in horned headdress and buffalo robe richly decorated with quills and fringes, had a special request of his white visitors. In celebration of the treaty, would Man-who-runs-like-the-Deer be willing to compete in a foot-race with the champion runner of all the assembled Indian tribes?

Harney promptly accepted the challenge.

Everyone adjourned to the open prairie outside the village stake enclosure. The course was set over half a mile of level ground covered by very short grass. Harney was introduced to the Indian racing champion, a lean Crow warrior named White Sun, and the two men shook hands.

The Crow wore nothing but a breechclout and moccasins. Harney nonchalantly prepared to race in his uniform, not even bothering to shed his shirt. A little weary from the long day's journey, and the struggle with O'Fallon, he was nevertheless brashly confident that the Indian didn't live who could out-race him. He did not even bother to remove from his pockets a few Indian trinkets he had bought en route.

To his chagrin, White Sun crossed the finish line one full stride ahead of him. The tribes roared jubilantly.

Harney ruefully congratulated the first Indian runner who had ever beaten him, then asked if White Sun would agree to race him again the following day. The proud Crow nodded.

The following morning the prairie was crowded with thousands of Indians and the regiment of the First Infantry. Some tribes piled up buffalo robes, ornaments, and tobacco as trophies to reward the winner of what all considered a race to determine whether the red man or white man was the swiftest athlete in America.

This time Harney did not make the mistake of underestimating the fleet-footed Crow champion. When he kneeled beside the almost-naked White Sun at the starting line, he wore only thin linen Army trousers and moccasins. The chief of the Mandans, carrying a lance decorated with eagle feathers, started the racers off by dropping an arrow.

To the thumping of tom-toms and the mingled roars of Indians and soldiers, the two contestants flew off along the prairie. White Sun led for about a hundred yards. Harney lengthened his stride, slowly closing the gap between them. As he began to pass the Crow, White Sun put on a burst of speed, pulling ahead again by three lengths.

Now Harney began to exert every ounce of effort. Sweat flooded out of his pores as he drove his legs in a pounding rhythm of giant strides. He began to overtake White Sun once more. Wild screeches and thunderous yells deafened him as he edged up to the heels of the fleet Indian.

White Sun turned on a fresh burst of speed.

Holding his stride, Harney gradually drew abreast of the red man, then began inching ahead of him. White Sun made a last desperate effort to regain the lead, lurching forward.

Pounding steadily toward the finish line, Harney felt

his breast snap the piece of deer thong stretched between two spears. He flew across the finish line a good four feet ahead of his now-staggering rival.

A mighty roar flooded across the prairie.

"I wouldn't have had you lose that race for a thousand dollars!" General Atkinson exclaimed enthusiastically.

Harney hoped that Washington and London would feel the same way when they learned about the ransom they had promised the Foxes for freeing the prisoners. It was cheaper, at any rate, than the price the American government would have had to pay for burying and replacing the First Infantry.

Go West, Red Man, Go West

Mission completed, the regiment started the return journey south in the late afternoon. When they reached Council Bluffs, they found the new Fort Atkinson well under construction. Welcome news awaited Lieutenant Bill Harney—word that he had been promoted to the rank of Captain, on the recommendation of General Atkinson.

A retired Army general named Ashley, who operated trading boats on the Yellowstone, called at Old Council Bluffs to see Harney when he heard that the expedition had returned. He had a proposition to offer the Army officer whose athletic prowess was earning him a favorable reputation among the Indians. If Harney would leave the Army to work for him, Ashley would put him in charge of a trading expedition to the Yellowstone. He would get half the profits and would not have to invest a cent of his own capital.

The proposal was tempting to the twenty-five-year-old Army captain who had no money except his meager soldier's pay. But he felt that the Indian Territory had more than enough traders already, thanks to John Jacob Astor. He could be of more service to the government, to decent traders like Ashley, and to the Indians, by helping to keep the peace as an infantry officer. He stayed with the regiment.

The regiment reached Jefferson barracks in October. After a short respite in St. Louis, it was ordered to Georgia because of new trouble with the Creeks. Chiefs of the Creek nation were refusing to recognize a treaty signed without their authority by a few bribed leaders. It required all Creeks to give up their lands and emigrate west of the Mississippi to what is now Oklahoma.

For almost a year, Harney's regiment protected white settlements in the territory, suppressing the outbreak of a full-scale Creek war. The trouble subsided when Washington reluctantly agreed to abrogate the illegal treaty, reducing the territory it demanded that the Creeks give up, and permitting them to remain in Georgia until 1827.

In June 1826, Harney's regiment was ordered to New Orleans. One day a new friend he had made, the Duke of Saxe-Weimer, took him to the Old Absinthe House on Bourbon Street, a favorite haunt of bayou pirates.

Their table was approached by an extremely handsome man, somewhat heavy-set, with broad shoulders and a dashing mustache. He was attired like a Southern gentleman of fashion, a beautifully ornamented sword curving at his side.

When the Duke introduced him, Harney blinked in surprise. The elegant dandy proved to be the notorious pirate, Jean Lafitte, whose three ships Harney had captured in the Bay of Atchafalaya eight years earlier. With a smile, Lafitte expressed the hope that the young officer had since given up harassing honest shipowners and driving their trade out of the Gulf of Mexico. Harney, in turn, hoped that Lafitte had since found better sources of supply than the cargoes of American vessels on the high seas.

In June 1827, he was once more detailed to the staff of General Atkinson, who was being sent to Wisconsin to enforce the removal of the Winnebago Indians west to Iowa. The Winnebagoes' resistance had the same origin as that of the Creeks. A few Winnebago leaders had been bribed into signing a treaty binding the whole Winnebago nation.

The entire area was seething with Indian unrest. Sioux Chief Red Bird was on the warpath against the white settlements for bribing Chippewas to attack the Sioux. Red Bird and Black Hawk, a Sauk leader of the Thunder clan, had raided two keelboats carrying stores to Fort Snelling, capturing their stores and massacring all hands aboard.

Black Hawk was a rebel bitter at Sauk head chief Keokuk, whom he scorned as a "white man's Indian." He was enraged by Keokuk's refusal to repudiate an 1804 treaty that General William Henry Harrison had tricked three Sauk clan chiefs into signing, after first making them drunk. They had ceded to the government all Sauk land in northwest Illinois for a small sum of money and a promise that the Sauks would be allowed to continue hunting and planting corn on this land—a promise the government had repudiated.

In September 1827, Harney led regulars and militia under Atkinson against the Winnebagoes, who were quickly subdued. Wheeling suddenly against a Sioux and Sauk encampment, Harney caught Red Bird and Black Hawk by surprise. Both leaders were taken prisoner and held by Atkinson to be tried for the keelboat massacres near Fort Snelling.

Harney found himself impressed with Black Hawk, an angry-faced warrior who wore earrings and necklaces, and carried a hunting falcon on his left wrist. The Sauk warrior upbraided General Atkinson for citing Harrison's 1804 treaty as authority for American actions against the Sauks.

"My reason teaches me that land cannot be sold," he declared angrily. "The Great Spirit gave it to his children to live upon. So long as they occupy and cultivate it, they have a right to the soil. Nothing can be sold but such things as can be carried away!"

In a thoughtful private discussion with General Atkinson, Harney wondered whether, from an Indian point of view, Black Hawk wasn't right. Certainly the fact that his fighting forces were inferior to the white man's didn't make him wrong. But Atkinson had long ago given up trying to decide the rights and wrongs of the Indian question. He reminded Harney that the only sphere of a soldier's authority was to carry out the decisions of the government.

Atkinson's answer did not satisfy him. Did patriotism require him to carry out the government's orders blindly, even when they were blatantly unjust or involved the extermination of an entire Indian nation?

At the close of the Wisconsin campaign, the brigade returned to Jefferson Barracks in St. Louis. Harney's troubled thoughts dissolved in a gay shower of social invitations that came his way. His rugged good looks, handsome physique, and attractive personality made him a great favorite in the city's drawing-rooms and at the incessant balls. One young Frenchwoman, Octavia LaVert, set her cap for him, but at twenty-seven Bill Harney was not yet ready to settle down.

In November, he received a leave of absence to visit his family in Tennessee. Afterward he visited New York City, then a bustling young metropolis crowded with ships in the harbor unloading immigrants, neat brick buildings close together, and wagons and carriages clattering on cobbled streets. He was amused at the way people rushed about so busily, hoarding time as though each passing moment were solid gold.

At his hotel, he met another young Army officer on leave, William Jenkins Worth, a devotee of General Winfield Scott. One day he and Worth began disputing the relative merits of Scott and General Gaines, both of whom were considered leading contenders to become Commander-in-Chief of the Army (known today as Chief of Staff) when General Alexander Macomb retired.

"Begad, sir," Worth snapped, "it would be an absolute catastrophe if General Scott were not appointed!"

"On the contrary," Harney argued. "Unless General Gaines wins the post, *Scott* will be the catastrophe!"

This trivial exchange of differences was to have far-reaching consequences for Bill Harney. Worth saw to it that the conversation reached the ears of General Scott, perhaps to prove his value as a heresy-hunter. Scott made a grim note of the name of Captain William Harney, whom he knew to be a protégé of General Andrew Jackson.

Scott hated Jackson, who had once called him a "hector-ing bully." An ardent Whig, Scott also loathed Jackson's Democratic politics with a ferocity that encompassed all Jackson supporters—especially General Edmund P. Gaines. Under Gaines's name on Scott's blacklist went a new one he would deal with in due time—Captain William Harney.

In June 1828, Harney was transferred to Fort Winne-bago on Green Bay in Wisconsin, in anticipation of fresh trouble with the Sauks and Foxes. Red Bird had died in prison, but after a year of being held for trial for the keel-boat massacres, Black Hawk had been freed for lack of evi-dence. He was now back in Wisconsin, reported to be stir-ring up a great Indian war against settlers in the territory.

At Fort Winnebago, which was little more than a stock-ade of twenty-foot loopholed logs built around maple-log barracks, a new second lieutenant was assigned to Harney's company. He was a likable young Kentuckian, fresh out of West Point—Jefferson Davis. The two men became close friends, often hunting together with Harney's hounds in the woods around Green Bay. Wild game, with fresh vegetables raised in the company garden, relieved the se-vere diet that wilderness troops were compelled to subsist on.

One day after the garden beds had been carefully spaded and raked, one of Harney's hounds broke into them. He raced after it with a yell of anger using, as Jeff Davis later recalled the incident, "language not suited to the pulpit."

The frightened dog ran across the garden and escaped through a gap in the fence. Harney cleared the fence at one bound. The dog raced up a long slope desperately. But with all the speed it could muster, it was no match for the long-legged Man-who-runs-like-the-Deer. Harney captured the culprit after a spirited chase, and administered a thorough walloping to its nonbarking end.

During the winter of 1829–30, Harney bivouacked with his troops at Portage-des-Sioux. They built rafts on the frozen-over Fox River, loading them with chopped logs. When the spring thaw set in, the rafts would begin floating the logs down to the fort. It was bitterly cold work, but Harney kept up morale by joking with his men, swinging an axe beside them, and challenging them to foot races on the ice. He was popular with both the troops and friendly Indian scouts attached to his company as runners.

One scout, a lean, bony Menominee named Little Turtle Egg, ran afoul of Harney when the troops returned to Fort Winnebago. Little Turtle Egg had violated a strict garrison regulation against theft by stealing another Menominee's tobacco ration. The traditions of the frontier Army required that he be made an object lesson of by being flogged in front of the garrison by the commanding officer.

Hating this idea as unnecessarily cruel, Harney tried to think up some way to avoid it without provoking criticism from old Army men under him. Finally, he summoned the guilty Menominee in front of the assembled company and led him out on the ice-covered Fox River. Assuming a stern mien, he brandished a cowhide-covered stick at the Indian and offered him a sporting chance. Little Turtle Egg would get a hundred-yard start. He would outrun his punishment if he was able to reach a bluff on the right bank upstream before Harney caught up with him. If not, he would be thrashed all the rest of the way to the bluff. The Menominee accepted gratefully.

The troops lining the banks of the Fox loved the idea. It appealed to their sporting instinct, and even the sticklers for Army discipline were satisfied. How could any Indian outrun Bill Harney in a half-mile race? Harney himself was sure he would catch Little Turtle Egg, but at least the arrangement would sharply limit the time he would have to administer blows—and no one could blame him if he missed his target often while both of them were running!

Both men stripped for the race, wearing only pelvic supporters and moccasins. At the crack of a pistol, Little Turtle Egg took off along the ice, trotting slowly for the first hundred yards of his handicap. At a second shot, Harney raced after him and the Menominee sprinted off at top speed.

The troops cheered noisily as Harney, flying along the ice with his sure stride, began to overtake the thin, lighter-weight Indian. A frantic look over his shoulder sent Little Turtle Egg suddenly cutting across the river obliquely. Harney pursued. The Indian raced light-footed across a stretch of ice he recognized as thin by its blue color. It cracked as he flew over it, but supported his weight.

When Harney came to the blue patch, the ice depressed, then splintered away beneath him. There was a loud splash.

He swam out spangled with icicles, mad as a charging bison. The soldiers howled with laughter. Little Turtle Egg, safe at the bluff, joined in their mirth. Then he faded away into the forest and prudently didn't return to camp until two days later. By that time Harney had recovered his sense of humor along with his body heat and could grin at his men when they reproached him for being unable to run as fast on water as he could on earth and ice.

The spring of 1830 ushered in vigorous new movement by settlers in the territory. Fort Dearborn, a federal post since 1803, was developing into the town of Chicago, and the first covered wagons were moving from the Missouri to the Rockies. On May 28, President Andrew Jackson, Harney's old mentor now in the White House, signed the Indian Removal Act. All Indians east of the Mississippi were required to move to western lands that would be given them in exchange.

Resigned to their fate, the Choctaws and Chickasaws began the long journey from the southeast to Arkansas and Oklahoma. The Creeks, whose experiences with Jackson in 1813 and 1817 had made them deeply skeptical of his promises of guaranteed territory in the west, balked and stood their ground, defying the government.

White settlers in Georgia had not waited for the federal government to order Indians out of their lands. As soon as gold had been reported in the Cherokee country, the Georgia legislature had passed an act confiscating all Cherokee lands within the state. The Cherokees had their own elected legislature and constitution, but the white Georgians declared all laws of the Cherokee nation null and void.

No Cherokee was allowed to testify in court against a white man or a white law. John Ross, leader of the Cherokees, pleaded in vain with President Jackson to rectify these injustices. In 1830, he appealed desperately to the Supreme Court, which ruled, "If it be true that wrongs have been inflicted . . . this is not the tribunal which can redress the past or prevent the future." The court had no suggestion for the Cherokees as to where to find the right tribunal.

Peace-loving Keokuk, now head chief of both the Sauks and the Foxes, sadly prepared his people to leave their Illinois villages for the westward trek. He urged the Sioux, Omahas, Iowas, and Ottawas to join the exodus. But Black Hawk and his followers, supported by the Foxes and rebels of other tribes, refused to go.

Soldiers and Illinois militia were sent into their villages to evict squaws and children while men of the tribes were away hunting. White squatters promptly moved onto their lands, in violation of the Treaty of 1804. Appropriating Indian cornfields, they plowed up tribal graveyards. Red men caught lingering in the area were beaten and robbed.

Black Hawk himself was set upon by a group of white settlers. They clubbed him so severely that he was lame and disabled for several weeks. Beside himself with fury, he warned the squatters to get out of the Indians' lands or die.

Holding secret war councils with disaffected leaders of the other tribes, he urged them to form an Indian confederacy against the white invaders. Most feared to join him, however, having no taste for war with the white man's powerful army. But rebellious wings of the Sauks and Foxes flocked to Black Hawk's banners. He sent some of his angry young warriors up and down the Rock River valley to frighten out white settlers by burning their cabins.

They appealed for help to Illinois Governor John Reynolds. He insisted that General Gaines, now military commander of the Western Department, come to the settlers' rescue. Reynolds promised to put thousands of Illinois militia at Gaines's disposal as quickly as possible.

In June 1831, Gaines marched a few companies of regulars, including Harney's, to Rock Island. Harney accompanied him as an aide to a council with the Sauks and Foxes, at which Black Hawk was present. Gaines was able to persuade a third of the chiefs to cross the Mississippi and join Keokuk, but most chose to follow Black Hawk. They supported his adamant refusal to be uprooted from their villages.

"You should know," Black Hawk warned the white officers, "that one reason we are resolved to defend our land is because our wives wish it. The Sauk and Fox women urge us to fight you rather than be forced to abandon our homes."

As before, Harney found himself strongly admiring the fiery Sauk leader of the Thunder clan. "Black Hawk," he wrote in a letter, "is a fine specimen of intellectual manhood, with a spirit of fun in him when he is not being outraged by what the white settlers have done."

Reporting on the council to Governor Reynolds, General Gaines emphasized, "Whatever may be their feelings of hostility, they are resolved to abstain from the use of the tomahawk and firearms, except in self-defense." He was hopeful that the arrival of the Illinois militia, added to his regular forces, would intimidate Black Hawk and his followers into fleeing across the river without a shot being fired.

His hopes were realized. On June 25, 1831, Black Hawk bitterly led the remaining Indians in Illinois out of their homes to cross the river and join Keokuk in Iowa.

Next day the ancient village of Saukanuk, which the Sauks had built to last for the ages, went up in swirls of flame and smoke. Even before the fires had died down, the sound of hammers and saws of the white settlers moving in could be heard by the sad-faced Indians across the Mississippi. A new white man's town began to arise on the site where the city of Rock Island, Illinois, stands today.

Gaines had refused the Indians permission to stay long enough to harvest the crops they had planted in the spring. Those crops, he promised instead, would be harvested by the white settlers and sent across the river. The settlers blandly agreed. When Gaines had pulled out with his troops, they promptly "forgot" this promise. To keep from starving that winter, the Sauks were compelled to cross back over the river and steal corn from their own fields.

Some were caught and shot in the attempt.

Black Hawk spent the winter planning a spring war to win back the stolen lands. He won promises of help from the Winnebagoes, Potawatomies, Mascoutens, Foxes, Sioux, and Kickapoos. Many Indian nations, increasingly incensed at their treatment by the government, were coming to realize that no tribe was safe. By 1830, Indian expulsion from the borders of white America was a fixed national policy. White men who dared defy it were treated as harshly as red opponents.

In Georgia, three white missionaries refused to recognize the legislature's right to destroy the Cherokee nation. Arrested, they were chained together and dragged twenty-one miles behind a wagon to jail. Two preachers who protested this outrage were chained and also thrown in jail. All were sentenced to four years at hard labor.

This was finally too much for Chief Justice John Marshall of the Supreme Court. He led a Court decision supporting the five religious dissenters, ruling that the Georgia legislature's destruction of the Cherokee nation was illegal.

President Andrew Jackson was beside himself with fury.

"Chief Justice John Marshall has rendered his decision," he exploded. "Now let him enforce it!"

Disdaining the Supreme Court's verdict, he signaled for the forcible evacuation of the Indians from the east to continue.

Bill Harney knew then that war was inevitable.

Black Hawk Fights Back

5

The Indian mood in the spring of 1832 was anything but benign. There was great bitterness among the tribes who had been forced across the Mississippi by white America's trickery, deception, dishonest and unkept treaties, and brutal use of military force. The Indian nations disagreed among themselves only on one crucial point—whether they could, if they united in a confederacy, wage a successful fight against the powerful United States to win back their stolen lands.

Rumors began flying through Illinois that Black Hawk had succeeded in forging this confederacy and was planning to recross the river at the head of a great Indian army. In actuality, only the Foxes had agreed to join the rebel wing of the Sauks in this desperate venture. But the two great tribes together were still a formidable threat to Illinois.

Harney and his company were now stationed at Fort Armstrong on Rock Island. From this outpost facing Black Hawk's encampments, he could hear a rising crescendo of war dances. General Atkinson, commanding the garrison, warned Black Hawk against starting any trouble. The Thunder clan chief sent back a defiant message. A worried Governor Reynolds sent out a new call for Illinois volunteers to join the regulars.

Hundreds of settlers began fleeing away from the Mississippi to Chicago, and there was even talk of abandoning that muddy frontier town. Neither side was actually eager to begin hostilities. Atkinson was worried because he didn't have enough reinforcements. Black Hawk fretted because the other Indian nations were reluctant to join the Sauks and Foxes.

He finally sent word to Atkinson that he was not trying to start a war, but only wanted the right of the Sauks and Foxes to return to their own lands to farm corn. If any bloodshed resulted, he declared, it would occur only as a result of troop attacks upon the Indians.

Setting out in canoes, Black Hawk and his men paddled diagonally upstream toward the burned-out village of Saukanuk. Without Atkinson's knowledge, an Army major named Stillman led 272 militia to intercept them. Black Hawk sent three warriors with a white flag to invite Stillman to his camp for peace talks. Stillman took them prisoner. Wondering what had happened to his emissaries, Black Hawk sent five more warriors to find out. They, too, were attacked. Two were killed, but three escaped to report back to Black Hawk.

Unnerved by their escape, Stillman panicked and decided to make an immediate surprise attack upon Black Hawk's forces. But by this time the enraged Black Hawk, encamped on the Sycamore, was steeled against any further surprises.

Although most of his band were out hunting for provisions, he hid 40 braves with him at the river's edge, waiting patiently for the attack he knew would come. Sure enough, Stillman and his 270 militiamen marched past Black Hawk's carefully chosen positions of concealment.

At a hand signal from the Sauk leader, the Indians fell upon the rear and flanks of the Stillman detachment, taking the white troops completely by surprise. The result was a panicky route of 270 disorganized volunteers by 40 cooly-led red men. It was a humiliating defeat for the American Army, marking the beginning of the Black Hawk War.

The news spread quickly. Black Hawk's runners fanned out to all tribes to tell their chiefs that the white men had dishonored a flag of truce, then made a treacherous attack upon the Sauks and Foxes. Black Hawk's victory over Stillman was argued as proof that his brilliant leadership could easily defeat the white enemy, if all the chiefs would unite their warriors behind him in a great Indian army.

News of the Stillman fiasco alarmed the white settlers, who began volunteering in new thousands for the militia. Professional soldiers like Captain Bill Harney were frankly disgusted by Stillman's stupid behavior. But there was no help for it now. Black Hawk and his followers were on the warpath, beginning to attack, plunder, and kill in the white settlements east of the Mississippi. Their nationalism was inflamed by Black Hawk's constant reminders that they were fighting a patriotic war to reclaim the homelands out of which they had been driven.

New Army officers were rushed to Fort Armstrong to

assist the fight against Black Hawk. One was a dashing colonel named Zachary Taylor, who became another close friend of Bill Harney's. Among the militia was a tall, gaunt lawyer from New Salem, Illinois, Captain Abraham Lincoln, who delighted Harney with his genial, earthy wit.

The three men—Harney, Taylor, and Lincoln—were soon inseparable, invariably to be found swapping jokes and howling in delight. They would have laughed even harder if anyone had suggested that two of the trio were destined to become Presidents of the United States. Or that another Harney friend, Lieutenant Jeff Davis, would end up President of the Confederate rebellion against the United States.

Fort Armstrong troops called Lincoln and Harney "the two ponies" because of the unique picture the two long-legged men presented when walking together. Their troops urged them to race each other, but Abe Lincoln knew better than to challenge Man-who-runs-like-the-Deer. He was content to rest his popularity on his warm concern for his men, his unfailing good nature, and his skill as a storyteller.

While he never pretended to be more than a civilian in uniform, he was never lacking in courage. That was more than could be said for a good many of the other militia officers. General Atkinson found them extremely reluctant to lead reconnaissance raids into Sauk territory. The memory of what had happened to Stillman and his men was omnipresent.

Asking Atkinson for fifty men, Harney promised to find out where Black Hawk's forces were hiding. The general, fearful he would be ambushed like Stillman, insisted that he must take three hundred Potawatomies with him.

The chief of the friendly Potawatomies, however, wanted no part of a reconnaissance mission against Black Hawk. So Harney, shrugging, set out with just the fifty troops he felt he needed, plus a few Menominee scouts. When Black Hawk's trail was discovered, the Menominees urged a retreat. Harney refused. The Menominees abruptly vanished.

Harney tracked the Sauks to an old trading post near the bank of the Wisconsin River, then sent back word to General Atkinson. Two attacking forces promptly went out from Fort Armstrong, one under General Henry Dodge, the other under Colonel Zachary Taylor. Harney and his men joined Taylor, fighting beside a company led by Captain Abe Lincoln.

The climactic battle of Bad-Ax took place in the reaches of rolling prairie and slopes of timber bottom, where rain-washed shrubbery stood against a limitless blue sky.

Black Hawk accepted the Army's challenge. Mounted upon his war pony and brandishing a spear-flag of feathers, he led his warriors in a series of fierce attacks and skirmishes, narrowly escaping death several times. There were gallant headlong charges and countercharges. Red men and white men met in face-to-face clashes, bayonet to lance, revolver to tomahawk. Indians overtaken as they scalped fallen soldiers would themselves be shot and scalped.

American infantrymen poured forth deadly volleys from their long rifles and were answered by Indian muskets. Dust and powder smoke swirled over the battle-grounds, mingled with the hoarse shouts of soldiers, the shrill whoops of Indian and the neighing of mounts. Bill

Harney's men followed him blindly into the thickest pockets of battle.

The tide of the fighting swung back and forth as first one side, then the other, gained temporary advantage. Finally, the Indians began to give ground. Black Hawk frantically called upon his warriors to stand and fight. They kept up a blazing line of fire until their ranks were scattered by a last furious troop onslaught that swept them back toward the river. Trapped between Atkinson's attacking forces and the armed river steamer *Warrior* now firing at his rear, Black Hawk waged a desperate three-hour battle for survival.

Hundreds of Sauk and Fox women who were with the tribes were driven into the Mississippi. As they struggled in the river, many were picked off by Army sharpshooters on the *Warrior*, who later professed to have been unable to distinguish them from their fighting husbands and fathers.

Black Hawk himself fled, but was captured two days later by some Sioux working with the Army. He was brought to Fort Atkinson by Lieutenant Jeff Davis. Even in chains, he presented a proud and imposing figure in his necklace of bear claws and headdress of red-dyed horsehair tied to the scalp lock of his shaved and painted head.

Some angry white settlers who were present at the fort demanded that he be promptly strung up as a "bad Injun." But General Winfield Scott, who had just arrived at the fort, ordered Black Hawk held as a hostage to compel the Sauks and Foxes to abandon their resistance.

Sent east under guard, Black Hawk was given an audience with President Jackson, who manifested great curiosity about the legendary Indian firebrand.

"We did not expect to conquer the whites," Black Hawk told the President. "I took up the hatchet to revenge injuries which my people could no longer endure. Had I borne them without striking, my people would have said, 'Black Hawk is a woman; he is too old to be chief; he is no Sauk.'"

Jackson forced the Sauks and Foxes, as well as the Winnebagoes, to sign a new treaty pledging to cede all their lands south of the Wisconsin and east of the Mississippi, in exchange for a reservation west of the Ohio.

Then he decided to parade Black Hawk through the cities of the East as a war trophy of the Jackson Administration. The unpredictable public, however, cheered the Sauk chief as a romantic hero of the wilderness war. Black Hawk returned west utterly confused about the nature of the white man who persecuted him one moment and acclaimed him the next. He settled down disconsolately on the new Sauk reservation under the rule of Keokuk, whom Jackson rewarded for his pacifist policy by declaring him sole chief of the Sauk nation.

Black Hawk's defeat brought in its wake a flood of new attempts by white exploiters to get rich at the expense of the Indians. In 1835, according to a report by the House Committee on Public Lands, Wisconsin lands rich in lead and other minerals that had been seized from the Indians were sold at private sale before even being publicly listed.

That same year Colonel John Milton told the War Department, "Many of the Creek Indians are almost starved, and suffer immensely for the things necessary to the support of life. . . . They have been corrupted by white men who live among them, who induce them to sell to as many different individuals as they can, and then cheat them out of the proceeds."

The men involved included leading Georgia and Alabama planters, politicians, and business agents.

Congress, at that time representing primarily the commercial and land-holding classes of white America who were shaping the government's Indian policy, ignored 425 pages of such testimony by the House Committee on Public Lands.

After the close of the Black Hawk War, Captain Bill Harney was granted two months' leave in St. Louis. Almost thirty-three now and feeling somewhat bored with his rootless existence, he began to think of marriage. During a nine-year friendship with the family of French philanthropist John Mullanphy, he had kept his eye on Mullanphy's pretty daughter Mary, who had blossomed into an eye-catching St. Louis belle.

When he proposed to her, he found to his astonishment that she had made up her mind to marry him when he had first been posted to Jefferson Barracks from Pensacola. The wedding took place on January 27, 1833, and the newlyweds took their honeymoon in Washington, D. C. On May 1, Mary was thrilled to be invited to call with her bridegroom at no less a distinguished mansion than the White House.

Glad to see the young aide of his Pensacola days, President Andrew Jackson decided he could use officers of that caliber around him in Washington. So Harney suddenly found himself an Army paymaster with the rank of Major. He was pleased with the promotion and increased pay, which Mary assured him was essential to furnish their new quarters in the capital in even the most Spartan taste. But he soon found himself chafing at his removal from a field command.

He resented the stigma attached to Army paymasters, who were widely considered educated men with civil careers ruined by drink, leaving them with only the Army to turn to. When the payroll was late arriving at a garrison, troops sang, "They say some disaster befell the paymaster."

Harney reflected wryly how swiftly and easily promotion came in the rear areas, safely distant from hurled spears and burning arrows, while line officers sweated out daily hardships and dangers for years with no visible sign of appreciation from the government they served.

The next year the first of their three children—John—was born. He soon had two sisters, Eliza and Anna.

In 1834, fresh trouble broke out with the Seminoles in the Everglades. The government had insisted that the remnants of the Five Civilized Tribes—Cherokees, Chickasaws, Choctaws, Creeks, and Seminoles—must be cleared out of the East to protect them against the hostility and encroachments of the white settlers. Some iconoclastic critics wondered why the government couldn't protect the Five Civilized Tribes by moving the uncivilized white settlers west instead.

To facilitate this final emigration of red men, on June 30, 1834, Congress set up a Department of Indian Affairs, and also an official Indian Territory west of the Mississippi. On October 28, the Seminoles were ordered to get out of Florida. The Creeks had already gone from Georgia

—now it was the turn of the last holdouts on the eastern seaboard. Only four thousand Seminoles had survived the first Florida war. But this stubborn little tribe refused to go.

They were especially outraged by the government regulation, imposed by the South, that prohibited Negroes or Indians with Negro blood from emigrating with the tribe to Oklahoma. All Negroes or half-castes had to be given up to be sold into slavery. This law meant the splitting up of many Seminole families who had been intermarrying with Negro fugitives for the previous two decades.

Determined to resist, the Seminoles plunged deeper into the swamps to fight to the death against the white invaders —both troops and slave-catchers. They had no central government like the Cherokees, but they shared a common Creek heritage of language, religion and customs. Strongly individualistic, they federated only temporarily in order to fight a common enemy. In 1834, the Seminoles united for self-preservation under the political leadership of Chief Micanopy.

It was Osceola, however, who emerged as the fighting leader of the struggle against white America. This lantern-jawed Seminole was an ambitious, hard-drinking brave who had already distinguished himself by bringing down many of Jackson's forces with his musketry in the First Seminole War.

In April 1835, General Wiley Thompson called a council of Seminole chiefs at Fort Gibson, urging the holdouts to sign the treaty requiring them to migrate west. Many chiefs remained ominously silent. Finally, Osceola approached the table on which the treaty lay. Pulling out his hunting knife, he stabbed it contemptuously into the fool-scap that was almost wholly bare of Seminole signatures.

He accused the white men of not only bribing and cheating them and driving them out, but also forcing them to sign a paper that made it right for them to do these things. He refused, warning he would arouse his people and fight the whites until the whole territory became a vast graveyard.

Thompson, appalled at the impact of this defiance upon the other Seminole chiefs, shouted orders for his arrest.

Osceola was seized and put in irons. Apparently chastened and repentant, he then humbly admitted that he had changed his mind. If the American general would free him, he would do all in his power to persuade other Seminole chiefs that resistance was futile. Thompson released him.

Under the pretext of visiting Seminole villages to win over clan chiefs to the treaty, Osceola organized a clandestine mass withdrawal of the Seminoles deep into the swamps. So began the seven year Second Seminole War, involving every regiment of the Regular Army, along with sailors, marines, and fifty thousand volunteer troops and militia. Opposing this huge force were fewer than twenty-five hundred determined Seminole warriors committed to fighting for their homes.

Knowing well that frontal clashes would be suicidal, Osceola split up his forces into small guerrilla bands. They operated by making surprise attacks on large American Army concentrations, withdrawing swiftly before they could be counterattacked. Osceola's strategy was a precursor of the guerrilla warfare that, over a century later, would enable Yugoslav peasants to thwart the invasion of Nazi Germany's heavily armed divisions; and also allow the communist peasants of primitive North and South Vietnam to frustrate the great military power of the United States.

When Osceola's forces began raiding white settlers' farms, many fled for protection to an Army encampment under a general named Clinch. He sent out a force of nine hundred regulars and Florida militia, but they failed to find any Seminoles to fight or capture. Hoping for a quick victory, the War Department began sending general after general into Florida.

General Richard Keith Call managed to locate and force a battle upon Osceola at the Ouithlacoochie River. Osceola was wounded, but the battle cost the Americans sixty-three killed and hospitalized. It was the first and last open clash of forces that Osceola permitted in Florida.

A large new expedition headed by General Gaines arrived in Tampa on February 9, 1836, but could get no closer to the wily Seminoles than a few trivial skirmishes. General Scott arrived to replace Gaines, but achieved no more than his predecessors. In communiqués reminiscent of the Vietnam War a century later, each new American general on the scene would announce the imminent collapse of Indian resistance.

Osceola would only laugh, and the Seminole game of armed hide-and-seek would continue, with Indian raids becoming more daring than ever. Whenever troops mounted a counterattack, Osceola would fight brief rear-guard skirmishes just long enough to let the bulk of his forces melt away into the swamps.

In December 1835, a major named Dade joined the search, leaving Tampa Bay with two companies of infantry and some artillery. That same morning he was ambushed from the flanks and rear by a large Seminole force that was led by Osceola himself. The whole detachment was massacred, except for two wounded men, who escaped by playing dead.

Osceola's daring even led him to infiltrate Fort King, pouring fire through the windows of a mess hall in which General Thompson was dining with his officers. Among the five officers killed was Osceola's chief target, the man who had humiliated him by putting him in irons—Thompson himself.

The news provoked shocked reactions throughout the country. A great cry arose that Osceola be crushed at all costs.

President Jackson, who found the Seminole resistance both humiliating and intolerable, decided to send to Florida the general who had helped him end the First Seminole War. So in the summer of 1836, General Thomas Sidney Jesup, the officer who had first commissioned seventeen-year-old Bill Harney as a second lieutenant, began organizing a fresh force of eight thousand new troops for a winter campaign against Osceola.

By this time Harney was utterly fed up with the tameness of his life as a Washington paymaster. Eager to return to service in the field, he told his wife that he had to join Jesup. His experience with the Seminoles under Jackson, and against the Sauk and Foxes, would make him invaluable as an Everglades scout against Osceola.

She knew better than to try to hold him.

War Against the Seminoles

6

The 2nd Regiment of Dragoons was being organized under Colonel David E. Twiggs. Through the Washington grapevine Harney heard that the second in command, Lieutenant Colonel Wharton Rector, was decidedly unenthusiastic about the prospect of leaving the capital to chase Seminoles in the Everglades.

He hastily sought out Rector to suggest a mutually desirable arrangement. What about changing places?

Rector thought the idea a brilliant one, even though it meant a step down in rank for him to that of major. He vastly preferred being a live paymaster to a dead Indian fighter.

On August 15, 1836, they went to see President Jackson at the Hermitage. When they came out again, Major Wharton Rector was a new Army paymaster, and Lieutenant Colonel William Harney was second-in-command of the action-bound 2nd Dragoons.

A few days after General Jesup had left for Florida, Harney followed with Colonel Twiggs. They reported to

Jesup at Black Creek. The general glowed at the sight of the thirty-six-year-old Harney, resplendent in his new Dragoon uniform with a new Colt Dragoon six-shooter in his holster. Jesup's eyes misted remembering the seventeen-year-old youth he had commissioned into the Army long ago in Baton Rouge.

He told Harney that his Indian experience would be invaluable for reconnaissance, since the hardest job in the Everglades was not fighting the Seminoles but finding them. No shrinking violet, Harney privately agreed with him.

Years later, in a letter to General Scott protesting against a lack of promotion, the forthright Indian-fighter did not hesitate to claim his due in the Second Seminole War.

"From the moment of my entrance into Florida to the day of my departure, I was active in season and out of season in the cause of my country," he wrote proudly. "I obeyed every call at any hour, whether to scour the Everglades at the head of small and inadequate commands, or to explore the dark, sinuous streams whose basky shores were the safe hiding place for the Seminole armed with his unerring rifle."

He added, "I was engaged in more affairs with the enemy, marched over a greater number of miles, explored more unknown country, was instrumental in capturing more prisoners, and was exposed to more personal hardships and dangers than any other officer engaged in the war."

This was highly egotistic, but completely true, as other letters from generals about Bill Harney testified. If there was any single hero of the Second Seminole War, he was it.

Jesup sent Harney to Camp Monroe to take command of three hundred recruits under a brevet lieutenant colonel named Fanning. When he arrived there Fanning, a veteran Army Officer, was greatly upset at learning that command of the post was being taken out of his hands. Feeling sorry for him, Harney asked the date of his commission. Fanning told him.

That settled it, Harney replied cheerfully. Fanning's commission predated his own, so that made him second in command. He actually preferred that Fanning run the regiment in order to be free to spend all his time in reconnaissance.

Setting off alone on a three-day scouting mission, he moved stealthily through the forests surrounding the camp. Eyes and ears alert for the faintest movement from swamps, lakes, and natural canals, he glided past draperies of moss hanging in graceful festoons from giant oaks and evergreens. Sometimes fifty feet long, these "hammocks" were favorite places of concealment for the Seminoles.

On one small island in an Everglades inlet he came upon some empty chickees—roofs thatched with palmetto fronds, open at the sides. But there were no animals visible, and the logs were cold in the white ashes of the cooking shelter.

On the second evening, while creeping silently through some palmetto clumps, he spotted firelight. Soon an Indian camp came into view. In the glow of cooking fires he could see Seminoles being painted in red and yellow—red for blood, yellow to indicate a warrior's readiness to die in battle. Some were also using a green dye under the eyes, reflecting the Indian belief that this enabled them to see better at night. Harney counted several hundred warriors.

Stealing back as quietly as he could and carefully avoiding observation, he told Fanning to set the whole regiment to work at once fortifying the camp with earth ramparts. They were going to be attacked, and recruits often panicked and ran before Indian charges unless they felt secure behind parapets.

Just before dawn on February 8, 1837, a sentry fired three warning shots. The dragoons spilled out of their tents into the firing lines behind their earthwork barricades.

A force of almost four hundred whooping Seminoles made both a frontal and left flank attack as the first rays of sunrise burst through the evergreens surrounding the camp. The battle raged hotly for three hours. The Seminoles' long, accurate frontier rifles were more than a match for the smoothbore muskets of the dragoons, but the earthworks kept troop casualties light. Only two soldiers were killed. Indian losses could not be estimated because the Seminoles dragged off all their dead and wounded.

In a battle report to General Jesup, Lieutenant Colonel Fanning declared, "Lieutenant-Colonel Harney, commanding the four companies of dragoons, displayed, during the contest, the greatest boldness and vigor, and inspired his newly-enlisted men with great confidence."

Irked to discover that Fanning had not yielded full command of the regiment to Harney, Jesup relieved him and put Harney in charge of what was now renamed Fort Mellon in honor of one of the fallen officers. In the weeks that followed, Harney put out peace feelers to the Seminoles. When Chief Micanopy heard that it was Man-who-runs-like-the-Deer himself who had repulsed his warriors at Fort Mellon, he agreed to lead clan chiefs, including Osceola, to a council to discuss a new peace treaty. Harney notified Jesup.

The pleased general sent word of the impending council to Secretary of War Joel R. Poinsett. An end to the Seminole War might be in view, Jesup reported, if only the white settlers of Georgia would let him alone. They persisted in attacking him for refusing to "convert the Army into Negro-catchers, particularly for the benefit of those who are evidently afraid to undertake the recapture of their property themselves." On March 6, 1837, Jesup left for Harney's headquarters at Fort Mellon to attend the council.

The Seminoles appeared under a flag of truce. Accompanying Micanopy were Osceola, Sam Jones, Billy Bowlec (more commonly known as Bowlegs), and other clan chiefs, along with large numbers of warriors and their families.

Micanopy announced that the Seminoles were prepared to go to Tampa for embarkation west at the expense of the government, provided one demand was made part of the treaty. No Seminole family must be split up. Runaway slaves who had married into the clans, and their children, must be allowed to go along on the exodus, and be admitted to the lands that had been reserved for them in Oklahoma.

When Jesup agreed on condition that hostages be offered as a sign of good faith, Micanopy agreed for the

Seminole nation and made himself one of the hostages until all his people could be brought together at Tampa Bay to board the ships that would take them to the west.

As the Seminole clans gathered at Fort Brooke, twenty-four transports steamed into Tampa to convoy them to New Orleans.

Convinced that the Second Seminole War was over at last, Jesup began dismissing the militia and volunteers, who departed for their homes and civilian life. The marines were sent back north, and the regular Army forces were pulled back from the malarial camps of the interior to coastal forts.

Harney was left with only a handful of men to round up slow or reluctant Seminole clans in the Everglades and to get them to Fort Brooke in time for the embarkation. The white settlers of Florida who had been frightened away, meanwhile, began returning to their abandoned plantations. With them came the slave-catchers, equally confident that there was no longer any need to fear Seminoles in war paint.

But as they waited for embarkation, the Seminoles grew increasingly homesick for the swamps and forests they loved, and apprehensive about the strange lands to which their chiefs insisted they must go. In June 1827, small groups of them began to disappear back into the Everglades. The trickle soon swelled to a flood. To his horror, General Jesup found that the whole Seminole encampment, with the exception of a few scattered clans, had melted away.

He confronted Chief Micanopy in mingled wrath and dismay. Didn't the Seminoles realize that what they were doing meant nothing for them now but suffering and star-vation? It was too late for them to plant corn for the win-ter. And those who did not die of hunger would fall in battle with the American troops. But Micanopy sadly ex-plained that his people had decided it was better to yield their lives than their country.

To complete Jesup's humiliation, young Seminole braves made a midnight raid on the thinly staffed post, freeing Micanopy and other hostages to slip away with them into the glades. Embittered, Jesup wrote to Secretary of War Poinsett asking to be relieved of the vexatious Florida command. But Poinsett felt that Jesup had gotten further with the Seminoles than any other American general. In-sisting that he remain, Poinsett promised to bribe a one thousand-man force of Shawnees, Delawares, and Kicka-poos to help him track down and recapture the vanished Seminoles.

Jesup fumed at the "damfools in Washington" who im-agined that hunting Seminoles in the swamps was like fighting other tribes on the plains. If the government would just be willing to keep the peace in Florida, he would have no problem. But he knew that even if he spent the rest of his career in the Everglades, he could never hope to flush out, let alone defeat, the elusive Seminoles.

Their only chance, he told Harney, was to get their hands on Osceola. He was the one, not Micanopy, who was the real core of resistance of the Indians in Florida. With-out his leadership the Seminole forces might collapse."

Harney offered to scout Osceola's whereabouts and try to seize him with a reconnaissance force. But it was the summer "sickly season," and Jesup would not let him reenter the glades until late fall or winter, when most military campaigns in Florida began. Jesup insisted that Harney, who was already suffering from malaria attacks, take a sick leave while he assembled a new army to go after Osceola.

So in August, Bill Harney left for St. Louis, where his family had now moved to be close to Mary's parents. Reunited with his wife and children, he gradually recovered his health in peaceful months of rest and relaxation.

His father-in-law, John Mullanphy, was baffled by the trouble with the Indians in Florida. He pointed out to Harney that the French had always got on well with those in St. Louis, and without the use of troops. Bridling a bit at the criticism, Harney explained that the government felt it could not develop the country properly as long as the red man stood in the way of progress. Mullanphy was not convinced.

It was, after all, really the Indians' own country. The French had always tried to behave like guests in America. In Mullanphy's view, the United States Army seemed to be causing more Indian trouble than it cured. Harney replied testily that he and General Jesup were only soldiers obeying orders. If those orders were bad, then the policy-makers in Washington were to blame, not the Army.

When he returned to Fort Mellon on December 1, 1837, Army forces had been strengthened in Florida by a cavalry force of militia and several thousand new foot troops. Harney joined Jesup in the field searching for Osceola. But they only found a Seminole clan led by Chief Tuskegee, and fought several fierce battles against his warriors.

By February 1838, Harney's reconnaissance convinced him that many Seminole tribes were seriously short of both ammunition and food. He urged Jesup to end the war with an offer of food and a promise to allow them to live undisturbed in the southernmost swamps of Florida where no white man had settled. Jesup pondered the idea, then agreed, but cautioned that Washington would have to ratify such a treaty.

This reservation, however, was not mentioned to the war-weary and hungry Seminoles, two thousand of whom welcomed a compromise that would allow them to remain in the Everglades. Osceola was among the chiefs who met in council with Jesup at Fort King under a white flag of truce.

Jesup found himself sorely tempted by his opportunity. If Washington did not ratify the treaty—and he had extreme doubts that they would—Osceola would once more slip through his fingers. He knew what President Jackson would have done in his shoes and decided that pleasing the President was more important than ethical behavior. In a sudden move he ordered his Fort King troops to seize Osceola, along with seventy-five Indians of his retinue.

This was the second time in Osceola's life that he had been put in chains by the white man, in violation of a flag truce under which he had been invited to negotiate. Disgusted at his own stupidity in trusting the white man's word of honor, Osceola pined away and died in a military prison only three months after his capture.

When news of Jesup's treacherous behavior reached Fort Mellon, Harney was sick with dismay. How *could* Jesup have been such a fool, let alone so unscrupulous?

The seizure of Osceola did not, as Jesup had hoped but Harney knew it would not, break the back of Indian resistance. The infuriated Seminoles retreated to their swamp homes. When the reply came from Washington, Jesup felt justified. As he had expected, his treaty was repudiated. The Seminoles were to be thrown out of Florida, and that was that. Word of this blunt verdict reached the Seminoles at the same time it reached Jesup.

The outraged Florida Indians returned to the warpath under the leadership of chiefs Sam Jones, Chaikika, and Billy Bowlegs. The Seminoles had lost all faith in the word of the white man. Now they were determined to die to the last Indian before trusting him again.

Jesup sent first a general, then a colonel with artillery detachments, after Chief Sam Jones. But it was Jones who found them each time, not they who found Jones, and the troops suffered severe losses. Finally Jesup ordered Colonel Harney and his dragoons onto Sam Jones' trail. Harney led his men on a series of rapid forced marches after dark, hiding and sleeping by day. One night they located the swamp village where Jones was hiding and crept up stealthily on his sleeping warriors.

Their surprise night attack was followed by a desperate battle. Sam Jones fled through a tangled morass into miry mangrove swamps at the rear of the village. Harney's troops were too heavily dressed and armed to pursue.

In the confused attempt to bring him down with standing fire, one dragoon, in violation of Harney's strict orders to his men, shot a squaw. Harney ran to her side quickly. The Seminole woman, dressed in colored rags sewn into a garment like a crazy quilt, was severely wounded.

He ordered an aide to build a fire to mark her position and prop his jacket on sticks to shade her when the sun came up. An Indian scout was sent to Sam Jones with the word of Man-who-runs-like-the-Deer that any Indians who came to rescue her would have safe conduct and would not be molested in any way.

Early the next morning, two Indians walked calmly into the clearing where the injured woman lay and prepared to carry her off into the swamps. Harney and a captain named Stowe watched from a copse where their troops had bivouacked.

One of the Indians was Sam Jones himself. Stowe made an instinctive grab for his gun; the capture of Sam Jones might bring the whole Seminole War to an end. Harney's hand gripped Stowe's wrist in an iron hold, immobilizing it. The chagrined captain reluctantly gave up the idea.

One month later, leaving his field tent in the morning, Harney found a beautiful multicolored Seminole blanket tied to the tent pole. There was a brief message in the Creek language that had been adopted from the Cherokee alphabet devised by Sequoya. "For Man-who-runs-like-the-Deer," it read simply. "From Woman-you-did-not-let-die."

The clan led by Sam Jones successfully eluded his pursuit, and Harney was forced to retreat to St. Augustine for new rations and supplies. Continuing to plunge through the Everglades searching for Jones, Harney discovered a large force of twelve hundred Seminoles led by Chiefs Tuskegee and Halleck Hadjo at the Locha Hatchee River. Bivouacking out of sight, he sent word back to Fort King.

General Jesup himself led the new forces that arrived to

give battle. Harney rode at his side. Caught by surprise, Tuskegee and Halleck Hadjo stood and fought.

Harney was the first to splash across the river into a direct hail of enemy fire. An Indian bullet narrowly missed him, catching General Jesup under the left eye and producing temporary blindness. At Jesup's agonizing cry, Harney wheeled away from the attack to go to his rescue.

The battle was a brief one, with the Seminoles deciding to take advantage of the momentary confusion to withdraw deeper into the swamps as quickly as possible.

Soon afterward word reached Harney at Fort Mellon that both Sam Jones and Chaikika were camped with their warriors in the upper regions of the Smyrna River. His first sergeant, a tough Army veteran named Koconski, selected fifty-four volunteers for an expedition. Harney led them down the Matanzas River in small boats until they reached the ocean. From there they attempted a twenty-mile voyage in the open sea to get to the mouth of the Smyrna.

It was early spring, and the waters were rough. All boats reached the delta of the Smyrna except Harney's own, which capsized in heavy seas. Entangled in a rope, he found himself drowning. He held his breath and floated to the surface. Struggling to free himself of the rope, he looked about for the capsized boat.

It was bobbing some thirty yards distant, a few of his men still clinging to it. He spotted a barrel of hard-tack drifting nearby and splashed to it. Strong currents swept him farther and farther away from the mouth of the Smyrna.

He felt himself being carried out to sea.

Massacre at Coloosahatchie

7

He knew that his only chance to survive lay in attempting the long swim to shore against the powerful ebb tide.

Working the coils of rope off his body, he pushed the hard-tack barrel away and threw his remaining energy into swimming for his life. The powerful muscles of his long legs helped him fight through the current and choppy waves that were sweeping him diagonally away from shore.

For almost two hours he fought the relentless sea until he was too bone-weary to go on. Only half alive and ready to give up, he suddenly felt sand beneath his feet. He collapsed gratefully onto a shallow sandbar, indifferent to the buffeting of the waves that rocked him back and forth like seaweed. Finally, twenty minutes later, he felt strong enough to dive back into the sea between sandbar and shore.

He staggered at last onto a narrow beach. After another brief rest, he hurried back toward the mouth of the Smyrna. If the rest of his men had given him up for dead, they would have gone on up the river. He was tremendously relieved to find them still searching the beaches for survivors from his boat. Astonished to find him still alive, they told him two others had managed to get back to shore.

After an hour's rest he joined them in the search until they were convinced there were no other possible survivors. Then they pushed ahead with the expedition up the Smyrna, propelling the boats by poles and oars until the river became an impassable swamp stream. Failing to locate Chaikika or lure him into an attack, they returned to Fort Mellon.

In April 1838, Major General Jesup was relieved of his command and ordered to the Cherokee country. He left under a cloud of criticism from Washington for having failed to bring the Seminoles to their knees. Angrily answering his critics in a letter to a senator, he pointed out that he had killed and captured in the brief period of his command twice as many Seminoles as all the other generals who had preceded him, combined. He also paid tribute to Colonel William Harney as the bravest and most effective officer of any rank to have served in the Second Seminole War.

His true feelings about being ordered to fight an aggressive war against the Indians, unleashed by his indignation at his Washington critics, came out in the letter.

"So far as I am concerned personally," he declared bitterly, "I hold in absolute contempt all honor derived from Indian warfare." It was a daring slap at President Jackson and all those who glorified the government policy of exterminating all tribes in the eastern half of the country.

Jesup's successor in Florida was none other than Harney's old friend of the Black Hawk War, now promoted to the rank of general—Zachary Taylor. The two Indian-fighters embraced enthusiastically at Cape Florida. Taylor told him that Black Hawk, a broken, disillusioned old Sauk of seventy-one, had just died on the reservation ruled by Keokuk.

But Taylor's really important news was that the War Department wanted to find out whether Harney was right in insisting that the only way to end the war was to let the Seminoles stay in the south swamp. General Alexander Macomb, commander-in-chief of the United States Army, had come to Florida with Taylor. He was waiting for Harney at this headquarters in Black Creek. Harney lost no time in getting there.

Macomb spread a large map of Florida on his desk as they discussed his plan. Harney encircled a southern portion of the Everglades, suggesting it as the site for an Indian reservation. Macomb expressed skepticism that Chaikika and Sam Jones would stay in the swamps and stop fighting. Harney pointed out that they were fighting only because the government had broken faith with them, after General Jesup had given them his word. The Indians were fed up with promises. And so, he admitted bluntly, was he.

General Macomb asked if the Indians would make another treaty on the strength of Harney's word. They might, Harney acknowledged, but he had no intention of lying to them himself, even under threat of court-martial. Before he made any treaty with Chaikika and Sam Jones, he wanted Macomb's personal word of honor that Washington would stand by it.

Macomb gave it to him, then sent word for all Seminole

chiefs to come meet with them under a flag of truce at Fort King. Sam Jones replied that twice the Seminoles had held council with the white man under a flag of truce, and twice Osceola had been seized during the peace talks. The Indians would come only on the personal word of Man-who-runs-like-the-Deer that if a treaty was not signed, he would supply all Seminoles at the council with guns, ammunition, and a three-day head start.

Bill Harney sent Sam Jones his word.

The Seminole chiefs came to Fort King for a council.

They agreed to stop fighting if they were allowed to remain in the Everglades in the area marked by Harney's crayon, at least until they heard from those Seminoles who had migrated to Oklahoma. Then, if they were convinced that their fellow tribesmen were prospering, they would agree to join them. If not, they would stay in the swamp reservation. The Army, meanwhile, must let them alone.

As a further gesture of good faith on the part of the white man, Chaikika asked that the government build a trading house for them on the Coloosahatchie River.

Macomb signed the treaty with an emphatic flourish. Harney gave the Seminoles his personal word that *this* time the Great White Father in Washington would honor it. Macomb promised to take it to Washington himself to make sure that it was ratified. Meantime, it should be considered official. He called off all military operations against the Indians.

Harney shook hands enthusiastically with Sam Jones and Chaikika, who praised him as a true friend of the Seminoles and all Indian tribes. He told them he would leave at once himself for the Coloosahatchie, taking with him thirty dragoons to begin building the trading house.

A steamboat was placed at his disposal, and Harney selected a site fifteen miles above the mouth of the river. He left two sergeants named Bigelow and Britton to direct the construction of the trading house, while he went on to General Taylor's headquarters at Tampa Bay to request two companies of troops to protect the new settlement.

Taylor refused them, pointing out that if the Indians were really pacified Harney wouldn't need them. He was also skeptical that "coddling" the Seminoles with trading houses was in the national interest. In his view, they should have been compelled to emigrate like all the other tribes.

Irritated, Harney replied testily and a heated argument developed. Their one-time friendship cooled in the exchange of words. Taylor flatly refused to give him the slightest help in either building or protecting the trading house.

Harney returned to Coloosahatchie in an angry frame of mind, hot and sweaty in the fierce July heat. His sun-narrowed eyes approved the joints of freshly hewn cypress posts and beams of the trading house framework going up. Three dragoons were nailing palmetto fronds onto crossbars for the roof. Sam Jones and Chaikika, he reflected, would be well-pleased. Now if Washington would only move just as swiftly, they could all be out of the glades by fall.

But he knew from his own experience in Washington that desk brass who had never lived on field rations or slogged through saw grass marsh or got lost in the endless swamps never had any sense of urgency about relieving troops who did.

Sweat pouring through his cavalry beard, he went to his field tent, removed his boots and coat, and lay down for a rest. He was getting the shakes again. Worn out, he dozed off almost instantly and slept through mess call.

At daybreak he was suddenly aroused by sharp noises that punctuated the glades. He sat up, blinking. Gunfire?

Then he heard the shrill Seminole war cries.

He leaped to his feet, incredulous. Without bothering about his boots or coat, he sprang toward the trading house in two giant leaps. Some of his men, half-dressed and un-armed, were sprinting frantically for the river.

Over his shoulder Harney saw three tattoed Seminoles with raised rifles racing through the unfinished trading house. One stopped to take aim. A bullet flew past his ear.

He plunged into nearby thickets, brambles ripping his flesh as he tore through them. Finding a clearing, he raced through it diagonally until he reached the river. Then he ran north along its bank for about a quarter of a mile. The Seminoles might track him, but he felt confident that they couldn't outrun him. Even at thirty-nine now, he was still as spry and tough-legged as a young buck.

Turning at a knoll, he splashed into the river. Then he walked out backward at a tangent and back up the bank. If the Indians who pursued him were credulous enough, they might believe that he and another soldier had plunged into the Coloosahatchie, and been swept to death in rapids below.

He rested briefly in a palmetto thicket. Hearing a volley

of gunfire, whoops, and groans, his mouth tightened. The commotion came from the point downriver where the trading boat was moored. Harney felt deeply sick.

It was incomprehensible. He'd seen Billy Bowlegs only two days before, when the Seminole chief had paid him a visit to watch the trading house being built. Billy had even brought him a gift of coontie root bread. What had happened in two days to make the Seminoles suddenly and angrily violate the treaty they had signed on May 17, 1839?

He began running again, heading toward a lumber pile his men had cut several miles from the trading house. Suddenly he heard a searching party of Indians angling toward him from the woods. He did not hesitate. Plunging into the river, he was caught up in churning rapids that slammed him along ruthlessly, half-drowning him. He felt himself hurled with bone-cracking impact against boulders beneath the foaming white-caps, and surrendered himself numbly to death.

Suddenly he was catapulted out of the torrent into a stretch of swift-flowing smooth water. Dazed, bloody, and exhausted, he managed a few feeble strokes to keep himself afloat. Coughing water out of his lungs, he looked around groggily. Spying a raft of drift timber that had lodged against a curved elbow of the river, he forced his way out of the midstream current. Ducking under the driftwood, he resurfaced among the trunks of rotting trees covered over with smaller driftwood.

Concealed from view of the river or its banks, he rested his head against the wet, slippery bark of one tree. He listened to the rushing noise of the turbulent rapids that had almost drowned him. Nearby a silvery fish flashed above the river surface. Then he heard them. A group of Seminoles had reached the river and were fanning out along it. He heard two Indians splash into the water, swimming toward the drift.

He waited until they had pulled themselves up on it.

Then, taking a deep, noiseless breath, he submerged beneath the water. Looking up he could see one Indian with a lance probing the driftwood. It pierced the space where his head had been a moment before. Then the probing stopped.

Moving with agonizing slowness even though his lungs were beginning to burst, he managed to get his nose above water and inhaled quietly. His eyes widened in alarm as he heard one Indian suggest setting fire to the brushwood.

The second Seminole rejected the idea as a waste of time. Man-who-runs-like-the-Deer had undoubtedly been drowned in the rapids, along with another white soldier who had escaped. They swam out in all directions, searching for his body as he watched them breathlessly through the chinks of his concealment. They frequently returned to the driftwood raft to rest and chatter. Finally, they left and moved on.

He listened to the sounds of the search party grow increasingly fainter. Then it was silent except for the sounds of the river and the wind in the cypresses. Cautiously, he waited until the sun went down. Taking a deep breath, he dove beneath the brushwood, bobbing up again in the river stream.

He staggered ashore and flung himself panting on the river's edge, his muscles jerking and pulsating in a spasm of exhaustion and tension. Later he found a small stand of crowded young saplings, pushing through them until he found a space large enough to permit him to lie down screened from view on all sides. Here he spent the night.

In the morning he moved on warily upriver, following the water but keeping at a remove from it. In the act of rounding a covert, he halted suddenly. Someone was coming along a woodland path. Harney took out his pocket knife and opened the largest blade. Crouching, he stopped breathing.

The other man moved out of the gloom of the cypress hammocks into a shaft of sunlight. Harney saw his haggard face.

It was Sergeant Britton, one of the few soldiers who had escaped by being able to swim. He revealed that Sergeant Bigelow and most of the others had been horribly massacred. The attack left him bewildered. The Indians had known the trading house was being built for them. Then why?

Harney was equally at a loss to explain it. All he knew was that Indians didn't break their word unless the white man did first. The two survivors decided to head for the protection of the nearest fort.

Their route was over mangrove roots and sour grass, which cut and lacerated Harney's feet. Britton, who had fled with his boots on, fared better. After a while Harney's feet were so torn and bleeding that he could scarcely move. Britton insisted that he wear the boots for a while, so that both of them could survive the torturous journey.

They came across the ashes of an Indian campfire. Harney blacked his face and torso with the charred wood, and Britton followed suit, both to ward off painful sunburn and make themselves less conspicuous. Reconnoitering cautiously, they continued pushing their way through the tangled vegetation as quietly as they could. Their course brought them to a winding bend in the river.

The sound of paddling and Seminole voices brought them to a motionless halt. Then Harney lowered noiselessly to the ground and inched through dense weeds on his stomach. A flight of birds flew screaming through the jungle as he startled them in their nests. Peering through some branches without touching them, he saw a cypress log dugout canoe drifting slowly down the shimmering Coloosahatchie. In it were three armed Indians, studying both banks for signs of movement.

Harney backed cautiously to Britton's position and whispered a plan. He would crawl out on the limb of a thickly foliaged fig tree that overhung the river. When the canoe passed beneath it, he would drop down, knife in hand, and upset the craft. He hoped to dispose of one brave during his leap, and go for the second in the water. Britton's task was to keep the third Indian busy.

Harney felt angry and desperate. He needed the canoe. Besides, Sam Jones and Chaikika had betrayed him. *Somebody* had to pay for all the dead men at the trading house!

He moved once more toward the river and crawled stealthily out along a thick branch of the fig tree. Eyes fixed on the Indian at the bow, who wore two diagonal ceremonial blood scratches on his breast and others on his arms and legs, Harney waited motionlessly for the slowly approaching canoe.

Two Seminoles held their rifles at the ready. In another

few seconds either he or they would be dead. His sympathy for the Indian cause blotted out in the passion of his anger, he beheld the approaching Seminoles not as warriors defending their homeland, but as treacherous savages who had repaid his efforts on their behalf with a senseless massacre.

He opened his knife blade and waited.

Then he slipped down from the branch noiselessly, like a great python dropping onto a passing deer. The canoe spilled suddenly before the Indians had time to realize what had happened. His knife flashed as the three red men hurtled into the river. The Indian at the bow gasped and died.

Turning swiftly, Harney slashed out in the water at the second Seminole. But the brave caught his wrist, counterattacking with his own knife. Harney locked his wrist in turn. They splashed and struggled for advantage.

The third Seminole surged through the water toward them, knife drawn. In a long dive from the bank, Sergeant Britton landed on his back. The Indian threw him off, whipping around and trying to stab him. Britton dragged him under the water. They fought furiously at the bottom of the river.

Harney, meanwhile, twisted his adversary's wrist backwards, causing the Seminole's elbow to bend. In a lightning-like move he forced the Indian's knife back upon himself.

Their arms trembled in a contest of muscle against muscle. Then the red man groaned, and his grip on the white man's wrist went limp. Panting and spent, Harney saw the current take the Seminole's body downstream.

Putting the knife between his teeth, he swam to Britton's aid. The sergeant and his adversary had surfaced in churning water, still locked in combat. The Indian's knife trembled an inch away from the white man's throat, forcing Britton's wrist back with superior power.

Harney fell upon the Seminole with his last remaining strength, striking down hard. The red man groaned and died.

The two bone-weary soldiers rescued the upturned canoe, which had snagged on a fallen tree. Then they staggered ashore and sprawled on the river bank, spent and wordless, remaining motionless for half an hour.

Finally, Harney stirred. All passion spent, he felt ridden with guilt and remorse. He had never killed a man with his bare hands before. It was not a good feeling. There was nothing brave or admirable about killing, he reflected disconsolately. General Jesup had been right when he wrote to a senator, "I hold in absolute contempt all honor derived from Indian warfare!" True honor lay in keeping the peace.

He and Britton paddled downriver in the captured dugout. A few miles farther they were overjoyed to come upon a boat with five men of the trading-house expedition who had also managed to escape. There were two rifles among them.

That might be enough, Harney mused. By this time the Indians would have discovered two barrels of whiskey, and would probably be unable to shoot straight. He was determined to go back to the trading house in case any of his soldiers might be alive as prisoners. When he asked for volunteers, all six of the dragoons promptly offered to go.

They reached a point downstream from the campsite by moonlight. Leaving two men with the boat and dugout, Harney led the other four noiselessly back to camp. They found the Indians gone, along with the detachment's weapons and supplies.

Harney counted twenty-one of his men dead around the camp area, scalps gone, bodies hacked and mutilated. His face quivered with grief and rage. He helped the dragoons bury their fallen comrades and held a simple service over them.

Sending Sergeant Britton and two men in the dugout to Tampa Bay to relay news of what had happened to General Taylor, he led the rest of the contingent back to his headquarters at Cape Florida. Here he found letters and newspapers in the mail packet that had missed him by two days.

Slumped weakly back in his chair, he read newspaper reports that explained why the Seminoles had broken their treaty and attacked the trading house on the Coloosahatchie.

Seminoles Don't Give Up

8

The treaty General Macomb had signed had greatly angered the white settlers of Florida, who were determined to force the Seminoles out. Although Macomb had won ratification for the treaty upon his return to Washington, as he had promised Harney, Florida's politicians had promptly sabotaged its enforcement by applying powerful pressure on the Secretary of War. Poinsett had hastened to soothe white Floridians with assurances the treaty was "only a temporary arrangement."

He had sent a letter to General Taylor to this effect, an obvious repudiation of the treaty. Once again the white man had made promises to the Indian that were cynically betrayed by his government. Made public, the impact of the letter had quickly embittered Chiefs Sam Jones and Chaikika.

The Coloosahatchie massacre had been their furious answer to Poinsett's treachery. They were particularly disillusioned with Man-who-runs-like-the-Deer. They had trusted him completely, and he had given them his sacred word that Macomb's treaty would be respected.

Now understanding the events at Coloosahatchie, Colonel Bill Harney was torn between deep gloom and indignation. Twenty-one fine men of his command had died because of the unprincipled perfidy of their own government. And because of Poinsett's cowardly and stupid capitulation to the white settlers of Florida, his own lifelong reputation among the Indians as a man of honor had been seriously tarnished.

Fighting mad at the War Department, Harney went to Washington to confront General Macomb. Even before the first angry words left his mouth, Macomb threw up his hands.

He acknowledged that Harney had every right to be furious, but not at him. The Secretary of War had given him carte blanche to make a treaty to get the war over with. Macomb had done so, but then Poinsett had reneged, and the whole project had collapsed. Macomb regretted that Harney had been misled, but insisted that so had he.

The bitter colonel then asked whether Macomb was prepared to prefer charges against Poinsett to bring about an investigation. That would force the government to make up its mind, once and for all, whether it really wished to deal honorably with the Indians or just exterminate them.

Macomb stiffened at the temerity of a colonel telling the commander-in-chief of the Army what he must do.

He bade Harney good day coldly.

War in the Everglades flared up again, now more savagely than ever. The Seminoles were fed up with government double-dealing. The white settlers, in turn, were outraged by the Coloosahatchie massacre.

Against this background, pressure on Secretary of War Poinsett by Georgia's politicians produced the final outrage against remnants of the Cherokee nation. On March 18, 1838, cold-faced General Winfield Scott invaded the Cherokee lands with seven thousand troops and a nonmilitary rabble of settlers.

Indian men, women, and children were seized and removed in wagons to concentration camp stockades for evacuation. Those who resisted were shot or bayoneted. Livestock, household goods, and farm implements were auctioned off to Scott's white camp-followers. They moved into the best Cherokee houses and burned the others.

From June through midwinter, fourteen thousand Cherokees were herded onto what became known as the Trail of Tears. Over four thousand Cherokees died during the excruciating hardships and suffering of a forced eight-hundred-mile trek to Oklahoma that lasted half a year. The government even charged the Cherokees with the cost of this forcible evacuation, deducting it from the sixty-four cents an acre "deposited to their credit" in the United States Treasury for the seven million acres stripped from their tribe.

President Martin Van Buren told Congress cheerfully, "The measures authorized by Congress at the last session have had the happiest effects. . . . The Cherokees have emigrated without any apparent reluctance." But an outraged Daniel Webster said grimly, "There is a strong and growing feeling in the country that great wrong has been done to the Cherokee."

As though he had not been responsible for outrages enough, Poinsett now ordered General Taylor to import

Cuban bloodhounds into the Everglades. They were used to hunt down the elusive Seminoles who, like water moccasins, glided through the underbrush and cane thickets with a slippery quiet that defied detection or pursuit.

Harney protested to Taylor that the idea was both horrifying and ridiculous. He proved right on both counts. The bloodhounds, trained to follow the scent of fugitive slaves, could not be persuaded to track Seminoles. Some who became lost in the swamps were even adopted by the Indians, who countertrained them to attack white pursuers.

News of their use finally shocked the press into asking some long-overdue questions. One sarcastic editorial asked President Van Buren whether, having failed to drive the rightful owners of Florida from their land, he had decided to tear them to pieces with bloodhounds and let them rot on it. Who was actually the savage and barbarian in America, demanded another paper—the red man or the white man?

The whole Florida fiasco, climaxed by the uproar over the use of bloodhounds, tumbled an avalanche of scorn upon the administration of Van Buren. When he sought reelection, it was one primary reason for his defeat.

Two years of uninterrupted Everglades scouting and fighting had proved too much even for Bill Harney's rugged constitution. In November 1839, he was given sick leave in Cuba. Mary and the children joined him as he rested and regained his health. Too soon for them, but none too soon for the restless Indian scout who felt like a fish out of water away from the wilderness, his sick leave was over.

He returned to his command in May 1840. It did not

distress him when General Taylor was recalled, another in the long list of generals who had failed in the fight against the Seminoles. General Macomb decided to take Taylor's place himself, but he could do no better. Next came General W. R. Armistead, bringing with him fourteen Seminole chiefs now in Oklahoma to persuade Chaikika and Sam Jones to join them in exile. This plan also failed.

Finally, in the fall of 1840, General William J. Worth was given command of the Florida campaign. He ordered United States troops to search out all Seminole villages in the swamps, then burn their shelters and destroy the crops on which they depended to keep them through the winter.

In December 1840, he summoned Harney and ordered him to find and take Chaikika. To aid him in his mission, Harney was given as a special guide a captured slave named John who had belonged to Chaikika's band, and knew where they were hiding. In the dead of night Harney led a force of ninety men in boats to an island in the Everglades surrounded by water up to five feet deep, and covered by almost impenetrable saw grass. He mounted a surprise attack at dawn.

The Indians organized a hasty defense as Harney swooped onto the island at the head of his men. But caught off guard, two Seminoles were killed and thirty-eight captured before hundreds fled into the saw grass. One who sought to escape was Chaikika. A trooper named Hall— the same man who had inadvertently shot the Indian squaw—recognized and pursued him.

Stumbling, Chaikika found himself facing Hall's rifle and flung up his hands in surrender. But Hall pulled the trigger. Chaikika fell lifeless into the water. Harney's search of the camp revealed thirteen Colt rifles and other goods taken from the force of dragoons under him who had been massacred at Coloosahatchie.

With Chaikika dead, Sam Jones and the other chiefs asked for a peace parley. General Worth stared in disbelief as a ragged force of a few thousand Seminoles came out of the swamps—ribs showing, barefoot, the women and children ill and starving—to the council. This was the force that had fought the United States Army to a standstill for seven years at a cost of twenty million dollars. The government had paid one white life and ten thousand dollars for each Seminole it had moved or killed.

The lesson was a costly one. This time General Macomb saw to it that the War Department listened to Bill Harney's views and gave up its attempts to deport the remaining Seminoles. Instead, the government finally agreed to live up to the treaty Harney had made and Macomb had had ratified.

Seminoles wishing to remain in Florida were given the freedom of the Big Cypress Swamp. The war was over, and the tiny, courageous Seminole nation emerged undefeated by the United States of America—an embarrassing fact ignored by most textbooks.

By March 1841, Harney's malaria had become so troublesome, complicated by respiratory ailments caused by long service in the hot damp swamps, that he was forced to take another health leave in Cuba. Not wanting to worry Mary, he wrote to her in St. Louis that his condition was "nothing serious." She promptly packed her trunks and, with their children, joined him in Havana. He swept up

John, Eliza, and Anna in a great bear hug and had Seminole souvenirs for each of them.

John was proud of his reputation as an Indian-fighter, and begged his father to tell him about all the Indians he had killed. Harney's face shadowed. He told his son about President Harrison, whom someone had once called an Indian-hater because he had fought the Indians in Ohio. Harrison had sued the man in court and won. He hadn't hated Indians any more than Harney did. Soldiers had to fight anyone the government told them to fight.

By December 1842, his health was restored enough to allow him to return to duty. The death of President Harrison in office had brought John Tyler to power. Tyler retired General Macomb to make the long-awaited decision between Generals Scott and Gaines for the post of Army chief of staff.

To Harney's chagrin, Tyler's choice was stiff-backed General Winfield Scott, the avowed enemy of Jackson, Gaines, and all their supporters. A vindictive man with a long memory, Scott had not forgotten Harney's contemptuous opinion of him expressed to Worth in New York City many years before.

Colonel Bill Harney's Army career now looked anything but bright. He tried not to be bitter as junior officers who had served with him in the Black Hawk and Second Seminole Wars moved up to generalships, while he, who had done more than any officer to resolve the Florida warfare, and who had served there longest at a sacrifice of his health, continued to remain a lieutenant colonel.

"Notwithstanding the service which I performed in Florida," he later wrote to Scott in an aggrieved letter, "at the close of the war officers who had not done one-fourth of the duty I had, were brevetted; some even received two brevets, and others, who had not even heard a bullet during the war, received one brevet." Scott ignored his protest.

For the next few years, he commanded six companies of the 2nd Dragoons on the western frontier, under Colonel David E. Twiggs. He had a twofold task: to protect the new Texas territory torn away from Mexico by American settlers from attack by the free-soilers of New Mexico over a border dispute, and to keep Indian tribes in that area pacified and off the warpath. In October 1845, he found himself stationed at San Antonio for a larger purpose.

President James Polk was supporting American expansionists who believed in "Manifest Destiny"—a presumably God-given right to extend the borders of the United States as far as possible, at the expense of the Indian nations, Canada, and Mexico. Polk insisted upon the right of the United States to annex Texas as a state and was spoiling for a war with Mexico over it in the hope of grabbing even more Mexican territory.

The rights and wrongs of the question confused Harney. He knew that congressmen like his shrewd old friend Abe Lincoln of Illinois had denounced Polk's moves as acts of unprovoked aggression against Mexico. But as a professional soldier, Harney could not ignore the fact that the Mexicans had assembled an army on the opposite bank of the Rio Grande, west of San Antonio. They obviously intended to attack the city he was pledged to defend.

Mustering a force of seven hundred men, he prepared

to march to the Rio Grande to prevent the Mexicans from crossing the river. One of his captains was unhappy with the plan because they had no artillery. Shouldn't they wait until they could at least get two pieces of cannon? Harney shook his head; there was no time. He asked whether the Mexicans had cannon. On being assured that they did, he decided that he would go and get theirs.

Holding the bulk of his troops in reserve, Harney crossed the Rio Grande with fifteen picked men. His new Aston Army pistol in hand, he walked into the Mexican town of Presidio and quietly captured it. Then he and his men hauled the Mexican artillery back to San Antonio.

General John Ellis Wool, meanwhile, had arrived in San Antonio to assume command of the military district. Hearing of Harney's unauthorized adventure, he sent an indignant order commanding the maverick Indian scout to return at once.

San Antonio citizens who heard about it were amused. One Texan informed General Wool with a chuckle that Bill Harney had a habit of not paying attention to generals' orders when he disapproved of them. Harney's failure to return immediately outraged Wool into issuing an order for his arrest. The general was mollified, however, when a few hours later Harney showed up with the captured artillery. Canceling the order for Harney's arrest, Wool held out his hand instead.

Harney ignored it. "General," he said quietly, "what the devil do you mean by ordering my arrest?"

The embarrassed general stammered that he had been led to believe Harney intended to disobey his order to return.

The tall Indian scout stared at him incredulously, then turned his back and walked out. Whenever their paths crossed subsequently, Harney always saluted as required, but persistently refused to shake Wool's hand.

By mid-May President Polk was insisting that Mexico had "invaded our territory and shed American blood upon American soil." This allegation was branded as a lie by both Lincoln and Horace Greeley, the famous editor of the New York *Tribune*. But Congress obediently declared war. Then General Zachary Taylor scored a series of dramatic victories by driving the Mexicans across the Rio Grande and occupying Matamoros.

Taylor's victories did not sit too well with General Scott, who saw them as Taylor's steppingstones to the White House. Scott, who intended to be Polk's successor himself, took the field as commander-in-chief of the Army to win battlefield laurels to advance his own candidacy.

Colonel Twiggs's promotion to general automatically triggered Harney's appointment on June 30, 1846, to full colonel. A major named Sumner moved up to become second in command of the 2nd Dragoons. When this development came to Scott's attention, he loosed a vengeful thunderbolt. Harney was ordered to yield command to Major Sumner, on the outrageous pretext that the junior officer was a "much safer and more efficient commander."

Fighting mad, Harney refused to obey the order. He challenged Scott to arrest him. "I had fully hoped," he wrote furiously to the War Department, "to share the dangers and deprivations of my regiment. If other motives, to which I dare not allude, influenced General Scott in this decision, he may arrest, but he shall not unresistingly degrade me. As long as I am a Colonel, I shall claim the command of my regiment."

Scott promptly ordered his arrest.

To the commander-in-chief's chagrin, a sympathetic court-martial board found Harney guilty only of disobeying orders, but not of insubordination. He was exonerated with only a mild rebuke. Scott was furious. In 1808, as a young officer, he himself had balked at orders of a superior officer, General James Wilkinson, and had been suspended for one year as punishment. Why shouldn't Harney be similarly punished?

But a second rebuke for Scott came from an even higher echelon—the White House. "You did not disclose a sufficient cause for the order depriving Colonel Harney of the command which appropriately belonged to him," Secretary of War William Marcy wrote to Scott at President Polk's behest. "The President deems it proper to apprise you of his opinion that Colonel Harney had good cause to complain of that order."

Fingers burned, Scott let go of what he now recognized as a hot potato. "Hectoring bully" he may have been, in ex-President Jackson's sarcastic phrase, but he was not fool enough to pursue his vindictiveness to reckless extremes. Harney was allowed to keep his command of the 2nd Dragoons. He was sure, however, that as long as Scott continued to wield the highest power in the Army, it would be useless to look for any further promotion in the service.

On September 14, 1846, General Santa Anna entered Mexico City as commander-in-chief of the Mexican Army. Two months later, Scott was ordered by the War Department to lead an expedition against him. In February 1847, Taylor defeated Santa Anna at Buena Vista. Scott laid seige to Vera Cruz a month later. Mounted on a clever white horse named Buncombe, Harney led the 2nd Dragoons in support of the attack on Vera Cruz.

Grudgingly acknowledging Harney's skill as an Army scout, Scott ordered him to make a reconnaissance of the approaches to the city. But he warned Harney against initiating any military action on his own. "Ascertain the strength and position of the Mexican forces on the Madellin River protecting Vera Cruz's supply line," Scott directed. "But remember you are only reconnaissance—not an attack force!"

Reconnoitering the terrain, Harney discovered that the main stone bridge over the river was heavily fortified. Mexican troops spotted his patrol and opened fire.

Harney fell back. The Mexicans gave chase. Ordering up his reserves, he wheeled and counterattacked. He scattered the Mexicans, then charged the bridge, routing its defenders. Two of his men were killed and nine wounded in an unscheduled victory that had sealed Vera Cruz's doom. Uniform dusty with battle, he reported back to Scott.

"I violated your orders, General," he admitted calmly. "We attacked the enemy and drove them back to Madellin."

Scott glared at the man who could disobey generals and be championed by the White House. He demanded an explanation for Harney's latest violation of orders. Harney explained that he had done exactly what Scott himself would have done under the circumstances. Since he was already under fire, it was simply a question of defending his forces.

Scott pointed out coldly that he could have withdrawn instead. It seemed peculiar that a military man with Harney's experience as an Indian scout had been so careless as to allow his patrol to be discovered.

Shrugging, Harney simply reported that by taking and holding the bridge they had cut off all supplies being unloaded by Spanish ships for Vera Cruz. Scott could now walk into Vera Cruz any time he wanted.

"I could have you court-martialed and shot for this, Harney!" Scott scowled. "But under the circumstances I'll be generous and say no more about it. Dismissed!"

Scott was as good as his word. In his communiqué no mention was made of the daring role of Colonel William Harney in smashing the outer defenses of Vera Cruz.

"What Did I Do Wrong This Time, General?"

9

Throughout the Mexican War the ungovernable fighting man from Tennessee was under fire in every battle except Chapultepec. In the confusion of the battle of Churubsco, Harney found himself pursuing huge forces of the Mexican Army with a mounted detail of only one corporal and six men. That feat, too, was studiously ignored in Scott's war communiqués.

A force of fifteen thousand men under Santa Anna, dug in on the impregnable heights of Cerro Gordo, barred the road to Mexico City. General Twiggs ordered Harney to scout the terrain for some way to storm up Cerro Gordo without being cut to ribbons by Santa Anna's artillery. Harney's reconnaissance found that the trees and bushes all around the mountain had been cut down, and the stumps sharpened to impale attackers.

He located an old stagecoach driver, Jonathan Fitzwater, who was married to a Mexican woman and knew every inch of terrain between Vera Cruz and Mexico City. Fitzwater revealed that there was a way to get up to Cerro Gordo, but that it couldn't be done by cavalry. Scouting the route, Harney ascertained that the stagecoach driver was right.

He asked Twiggs to be allowed to lead an attack on foot up a rocky and perilous slope at a rear flank of Cerro Gordo. Two United States Army engineers—Robert E. Lee and G. T. Beauregard—agreed that Harney's plan offered the only chance of a swift surprise victory. General Scott grudgingly gave permission for Harney to make the attack with his 2nd Dragoons.

Scott also ordered Lee and Beauregard to cut a road to the right of Harney's advance, so that artillery could spiral up the base of Cerro Gordo in support of the foot attack. As fast as the Army engineers could cut the road, Twiggs moved up artillery camouflaged by brush.

On April 17, 1847, in the early dawn, Harney led his men up the mountain. But the Mexicans discovered Twiggs's road and opened fire on the engineers. Harney continued storming up Cerro Gordo without artillery support.

Encountering two outposts on the mountain, he overran both and drove off three counterattacks. Scott rushed four infantry companies behind him for support. The battle on the mountainside raged all day long. By midmorning, Harney was still fighting his way up the heights. Santa Anna refaced his artillery on top of Cerro Gordo and began pouring down a murderous fire of grape, canister, and musketry.

During his worst moments of Indian warfare, Harney had never endured any attacks as frightening as this one. Pushing through the deadly barrage, he shouted an order to his men to fix bayonets. Then he led them in taking one stone breastworks after another in their fight up to the summit.

Scrambling up the mountain yards in advance of his men, waving his sword when he wasn't using it, he shouted a steady exhortation of encouragement. Withering fire decimated the ranks behind him. As soon as one man fell, others closed the gap, scrambling to keep up with their leader.

Harney and his men swept up and over the crest of Cerro Gordo. Plunging into the fortress, he found Mexican General Vasquez sprawled on his back, eyes sightless.

Harney pulled down the Mexican flag and raised the American colors over Cerro Gordo. A tremendous cheer rose from the plains below. Other American divisions followed up the steep north face of the mountain as Santa Anna and his men raced down the southern slope, escaping along the Jalapa road. The Mexican commander fled with only eight thousand men, the other seven thousand either killed or taken prisoner in the battle.

Exhilarated by the fierce fighting, Harney led his dragoons to horse on captured mounts. They chased Santa Anna and his troops into and beyond Jalapa. Sabers drawn, they overtook and slew hundreds of panicky Mexican soldiers in flight. When Harney returned, spent, filthy, and savagely jubilant, he found General Scott waiting for him on the heights of Cerro Gordo. The two men stared at each other wordlessly for a moment. Then Harney broke the silence.

"What did I do wrong this time, General?" he challenged.

Scott's antipathy warred with admiration. Finally, unexpected tears sprang to his eyes. Unable to speak for a moment, he clasped Harney's arms and embraced him.

"I cannot now express my admiration of your gallant achievement, Colonel, but at the proper time I shall take great pleasure in thanking you in proper terms."

Stunned by this uncharacteristic acknowledgment, Harney could only stare at him in disbelief.

The victory at Cerro Gordo, opening the way to Mexico City, netted the Americans forty-three Spanish artillery pieces and five thousand rifles, along with five generals and three thousand prisoners. When the smoke of battle died down, a Mexican officer was seen slowly riding along the foot of the mountain, sadly surveying the extent of defeat. American troops opened fire.

Ignoring them, the Mexican calmly continued his inspection. Harney ordered all firing to cease instantly and waved down at the enemy officer. As the American rifles fell silent, the Mexican raised his hand in a melancholy salute.

However much General Scott might dislike Colonel Bill Harney personally, or detest his ties to Jackson or Gaines, he could now no longer ignore the firebrand officer's conspicuous gallantry. On April 18, 1847, the hero of Cerro Gordo was breveted brigadier-general in the United States Army "for gallant and meritorious conduct."

His fame led the citizens of New Orleans, who remembered him fondly from his pirate-chasing days, to buy a magnificent horse and ship it to him in Mexico as a tribute. Touched, Harney nevertheless continued to be faithful to his mount Buncombe, who by now was almost part of himself in battle.

"Friends and Foes"

William S. Harney
(U.S. Signal Corps Photo [Brady Collection]
in the National Archives)

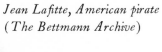
Jean Lafitte, American pirate
(The Bettmann Archive)

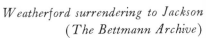
Weatherford surrendering to Jackson
(The Bettmann Archive)

Andrew Jackson
(The Bettmann Archive)

Zachary Taylor (The Bettmann Archive)

General Winfield Scott (Culver Pictures)

Harney's race with a Crow Indian
(Princeton University Library)

A soldier's discharge signed by A. Lincoln, Captain
(The Bettmann Archive)

Osceola. Painting by George Catlin
(The Bettmann Archive)

The capture of Osceola by American soldiers
(The Bettmann Archive)

General Taylor at Buena Vista
(The Bettmann Archive)

A pioneer wagon train
(Kansas State Historical Society, Topeka)

*Colonel Harney
at Cerro Gordo
(Princeton
University Library)*

Billy Bowlegs, Seminole Chief
(Kansas State Historical Society, Topeka)

*Father De Smet
(Princeton University
Library)*

*Harney with his
horse Buncombe
(Princeton University
Library)*

Jefferson Davis
(*The Kansas State Historical
Society, Topeka*)

General Harney as a
member of the Indian
Peace Commission in 1868
(*U.S. Signal Corps Photo
in the National Archives*)

He was placed in command of a brigade of cavalry consisting of the 1st, 2nd, and 3rd Dragoons. Scott used him for dangerous reconnaissance and scouting missions, knowing that Harney could always be depended upon to return with the intelligence needed, depite somehow always managing to find it necessary to fight a battle en route.

On August 12, Scott ordered him to ascertain the least fortified route into Mexico City. Harney once more sought out his friend Jonathan Fitzwater. The stagecoach driver advised him as to the most likely roads to scout. In the course of this reconnaissance, Harney encountered a Mexican detachment and could not resist chasing them through San Augustine, despite Scott's strict orders not to engage in battle.

En route to Mexico City, Harney helped force the surrender of San Pablo. On September 7, Scott ordered him to take the fort of Molino del Rey. When the 2nd Dragoons charged, they were driven back by concealed fire from the enemy's right flank. Puzzled, Harney rode forward alone to examine the position himself. The hidden Mexicans allowed him to approach within 120 yards, then opened fire. Harney calmly wheeled Buncombe around and retreated at a square trot.

"Gallop, sir—gallop!" pleaded a worried officer.

Harney only grinned and waved.

"The rascals never hit anything they shoot at!"

His cool example was not lost on the dragoons. Ignoring the Mexican fire, they galloped forward and took the fort.

On September 18, 1847, Bill Harney rode into Mexico City with General Scott and the victorious American Army.

He was quartered in a palace where the former Emperor Iturbide had been crowned, and his brigade was garrisoned on the palace grounds. Soon after their occupation, an American civilian named Hall, attached to the military, came to the palace to complain that his Mexican wife had been beaten by her countrymen as a traitor for marrying a *gringo*.

Harney bristled. His Tennessee upbringing made him outraged whenever women were treated unchivalrously. He had been equally angered by the mistreatment of Indian women in the Black Hawk and Seminole wars. Ordering the arrest of the offenders, he turned them over to some southern soldiers.

"There's my back yard," he snapped. "Take these brave fellows in and do what you think the occasion calls for. I won't interfere."

The dragoons entrusted with the prisoners flogged the captured men. Unfortunately for Harney, one of those punished happened to be a French citizen, not a Mexican. The indignant French government filed a protest with Washington.

Secretary of War W. L. Marcy sent Harney an official reprimand, adding, "It is painful to the President to censure the conduct of a gallant and meritorious officer like yourself; but a sense of what is due to justice and to the French nation requires this at his hands."

Reading it, Harney chewed on a cigar in disgust, then flung the reprimand in the wastebasket.

In October 1847, Scott dispatched Harney to Washington with important messages for the War Department. En route, he was astonished to find the whole city of New Orleans turning out for him in a thunderous ovation. Embarrassed and uncomfortable, he ducked the crowds and slipped aboard a Mississippi steamer. When he stopped off at St. Louis to see Mary and the children, he found the same huge mobs waiting to hail him as the hero of the Mexican War.

A coach with six white horses drew up at his home, captured him from his family and brought him to the People's Theatre. Pit, galleries, and boxes overflowed with people who greeted him with tremendous applause and cheers.

At Philadelphia the hotel where he stopped was besieged by enormous crowds blocking off all traffic in the street below. Harney thought nothing of this at first, because the city was preparing to celebrate the first return of its volunteers from Mexico. He went out on a balcony of his room to watch. Suddenly the streets roared with his name.

Realizing with amazement that the huge demonstration was for him, he backed into his room. Flustered, he closed the balcony doors. But the crowds kept calling for him, then burst into the hotel. Rushing up the stairs, they almost broke down the doors in their eagerness to lionize him.

Delivering the dispatches Scott had entrusted to him for the War Department, Harney was told that the President wanted to see him. Polk congratulated him and thanked him on behalf of the American people. Harney used the opportunity to put in a special plea for the troops under him.

Many had fallen in love with and married Mexican

girls, wanting to remain with them in Mexico. The War Department had decreed, however, that they must return with the American Army or be declared deserters. Harney protested that this was military bureaucracy at its worst, a poor way to reward young men who had volunteered to fight for their country. Polk agreed and promised to see to it that the rule was changed at once. It was.

The Mexican War over, Harney and the 2nd Dragoons were posted to Texas to guard the western frontier. He was granted a number of leaves to spend with Mary and the children in St. Louis. The Harneys were deeply worried because young John had taken seriously ill with some inexplicable malady. The doctor advised that travel abroad and a change of climate could be helpful. So Harney urged Mary to go to Europe with the children and promised to join them when he could.

In 1849, from his isolated command in Texas, Harney read that his one-time bosom companion of the Black Hawk War, General Zachary Taylor, had entered the White House. One week later the first load of Eastern goldseekers arrived in San Francisco aboard the steamship packet *California*.

Harney knew that the discovery of gold out west meant more trouble for the Indians. Their possession of the western lands stood in the way of the white man's greed, and so he was not surprised when control of Indian affairs was taken out of the hands of the War Department and placed under the civilian Interior Department.

There was a good reason for this change, he knew. The government had decided that the reason the Indians were able to "give so much trouble" was their unity as tribal societies and as nations. The new policy toward the Indians was one of "divide and conquer"—splitting them up into small weak groups, torn by dissent, so that they could not unite as Indian armies against the white man.

In 1849, a Congress intent upon expanding white America's borders in every direction selected the Interior Department as its agency for subjugating the Indian Territory out west, and transferring to private white hands as much valuable mining, timber, and grazing lands as possible. The new policy of the Bureau of Indian Affairs called for "civilizing" the Indians by training them for farming and trades—in effect a scheme to break up their unifying tribal pattern.

The bureau planned a new "land allotment program" that would divide up tribal lands among the Indians. Each family would get title to a small piece of land of its own, ostensibly to make them "self-supporting." Harney wasn't fooled. He knew that the real purpose of this plan was to weaken the tribes by breaking their bonds as communal hunters, trappers, and agriculturalists. Splitting up the tribal lands into small holdings would also let white traders and speculators easily buy them up for whiskey and cheap trinkets.

It was the same old story, Harney reflected bitterly— the government's attempt to use laws to rob the Indians for the benefit of a powerful clique of unscrupulous businessmen. Pressure on Congress to pass the land allotment proposal grew intense in September 1850, as California joined the Union as a state and New Mexico and Utah were admitted as territories. Harney had no illusions about what would happen to the Indian treaties the government had made, giving western territory to the tribes who had had their eastern lands taken away from them forcibly.

He waited for the inevitable new Indian wars.

Meanwhile, he was bored and irked by his Texas command. By the summer of 1852 peacetime had shrunk his regiment to little more than a company in size. He wrote a testy letter to Scott complaining that his thirty-five years of military service deserved better reward then a military backwater like Texas with "the paper command of my regiment and of a garrison of a single company!" Scott ignored the letter.

He had more weighty matters on his mind. The Whig party had finally given Scott his chance to emulate three contemporary generals before him—Jackson, Harrison, and Taylor—by winning the Presidency. He was embittered by an overwhelming defeat at the hands of Democratic Franklin Pierce.

Harney also became increasingly restless and irritable, showing it on every occasion. To bolster the sagging morale of the 2nd Dragoons, he had procured for them dashing Mexican sombreros of fine quality. One day in San Antonio, he came across a civilian wearing one of these same hats.

"Where did you get that hat?" Harney snapped.

"Why, I bought it from a store," the man replied.

"No, sir, those hats belong to the 2nd Dragoons alone, and the men don't sell them. Surrender that hat immediately or I'll have you locked up as a thief!"

The man hastily turned over his hat and fled.

On another occasion, while riding Buncombe in Austin, he was almost run down by a teamster. Wheeling his mount, Harney made several unfavorable references to the driver's ancestry. The teamster, a powerful man with bulging biceps, spit on his hands and leaped down from the buckboard. Harney smiled tightly under his beard. Slowly unbuttoning and shedding his tunic, he hung it on the horn of his saddle and dismounted.

The teamster landed the first blow. It caught Harney on the neck and staggered him. He fell back, seemingly stunned. The teamster leaped forward eagerly to finish him off. Harney sidestepped nimbly. As the burly driver lunged past, the shirt-sleeved general sent him sprawling with a powerful clout to the side of the jaw.

Waiting for the teamster to regain his feet, Harney slammed a left fist into his stomach, then a right to his face. He retaliated with two hard punches to the head, then bulled Harney backward by brute weight. Whirling sideways, the soldier let him lurch past. As the teamster recovered and swung around, fists raised, he ran into a powerful roundhouse that set him back on his heels.

Staggering under a rain of blows, he sat down. Thinking things over, he decided he had had enough and held out his hand with a grin on his puffing lips. Harney smiled and shook hands, then helped the teamster to his feet. Remarking dryly that he could always use a good fighting man in the 2nd Dragoons, he put on his tunic, swung back into the saddle and rode off exhilarated by the afternoon's excitement.

Secretary of War Charles M. Conrad sent a shipment of experimental meat biscuit to Texas, ordering Harney to test it out as a field substitute for meat and bread. Carrying out instructions, Harney sent a dozen officers out on a ten-day march with nothing but the biscuit, asking them to report back their opinion of it.

At the end of ten days, the windows of Harney's office suddenly splintered with several loud crashes. He instinctively dove behind his desk and went for his pistol.

Then he saw half a dozen of the hard biscuits lying on the floor among the slivers of glass. A thin, hollow-cheeked captain in a dusty uniform checked in with a salute.

"Report delivered as ordered, sir," he announced.

Harney fell over his desk howling with laughter.

The son of John J. Audubon, the famous naturalist, called on General Bill Harney for a bit of nonmilitary help. He explained that he was collecting specimens of fauna and needed a rare species of leopard. Could the general help him bag one? The general not only could but happily would.

The next morning they set out with a pack of dogs in a forest where Harney knew there were leopards. They treed one in a live oak, but it was so screened by foliage as to present only the tip of its nose as a target. Drawing a bead with his rifle, Harney tore off one shot. The animal didn't move. The tall general stared at his rifle sights, baffled. As he lifted the gun to take another shot, the leopard suddenly toppled out of the tree, dead.

"That beast almost shook my confidence in my marksmanship," Harney admitted in relief. The leopard proved to be the exact species young Audubon needed to complete his collection.

Occasional action came Harney's way when bands of Tonquas, Lipans, and northern Comanches raided Texan ranches, driving off horses, mules, and livestock. Harney led the expeditions after them himself. Fighting several skirmishes, he recaptured many of the stolen animals and brought back Indian prisoners.

One was the Comanche chief of the Burnt Meat band. He was captured tomahawk in hand, after a running battle during which a flint arrow ruined Harney's Mexican sombrero. A colonel rode up with the chief, turning over the tomahawk to Harney. The general hefted it, admiring its handsome carving and dyed deerskin strapping.

"Chief," he said, "we don't want to fight the Comanches. Why do you keep raiding the ranches?" He tossed the tomahawk in the air and caught it. "Why not bury the hatchet?"

The bound Indian on a handsome pinto extended his leg in the saddle, indicating Harney's scabbard. "Comanche bury hatchet," he said stonily, "when white man bury sword."

Fight or Shake Hands

10

When two fresh companies of dragoons arrived at his post for escort duty west, Harney recognized one private as an old former sergeant who had served with him against the Sauks and Seminoles. He summoned the veteran.

"Aren't you Sergeant Koconski?"

"I *was* a sergeant, General, yessir."

"Who reduced you to the ranks, and why?"

"Captain Newton, sir. For getting drunk."

Harney ran his fingers through his steel-gray hair.

"Koconski, you go back and tell Captain Newton you're a sergeant again. Any man who's served as long as you have, and fought as hard as you did, can drink as hard as you do!"

Koconski returned to his company and put on his old sergeant's chevrons. His commanding officer angrily demanded to know who had told him that he could do this.

"A sight better man than you, Captain," Koconski replied mildly. "General Harney." The chevrons stayed on.

The opening up of the west made Harney increasingly bitter over Scott's apparent determination to let him languish in Texas doing desultory border duty. Each time he saw a new opportunity for more active service, he hopefully put in a request for it. The Gadsden Purchase of December 1853 called for a railroad to be built from Texas to California. He asked to command a military expedition to scout the best route for it, guaranteeing he could do it without stirring up any wars in the Indian Territory. He also asked to be assigned to new western forts to protect the wagon trains now moving through Indian lands, confident he could protect not only settlers from Indians, but Indians from settlers.

His pleas for more active duty gathered dust in the War Department. In July 1854, fed up with garrison life in Texas, he applied for and was granted a two-year leave of absence to join his family, who were now living in Paris.

He was relieved to find his son John somewhat improved in health, and took the family to southern France to enjoy life on the Mediterranean beaches. Mary was beside herself with joy, scarcely able to believe her good fortune in having her husband to herself and the children for two whole years. They made ambitious plans for a grand tour of Europe and North Africa. Mary had never been happier.

But at the end of October, a bare three months after his reunion with his family in Europe, he received a communiqué from President Franklin Pierce's new Secretary of War. His old comrade and junior officer of Black Hawk War days, Jefferson Davis, urged him to return home at once. He was badly needed. The Sioux in the Kansas and

Nebraska territories were beating war drums over the white invasion of lands that had been guaranteed to them in earlier treaties. They were particularly upset by the vast increase of pioneer wagon trains moving through their lands, killing their game and often shooting Indians on sight as "savages."

Bill Harney rearranged his family plans as quickly as he could. He set out for Washington on Christmas Eve 1854. Reporting to Jeff Davis, he was clasped in an enthusiastic embrace by his admiring old friend. Behind closed doors they enjoyed a private reunion, exchanging hilarious reminiscences of the old Black Hawk campaign.

President Pierce summoned him to the White House. He apologized for interrupting Harney's leave and said he would not presume to order him back to duty, since Harney had already done so much for his country. But would he consent to assume the command in the west and to get the Sioux in line? Calling him the nation's best Indian-fighter, Pierce declared he trusted Harney as he trusted no other soldier. "In this," he added, "I know I follow a long line of Presidents since Monroe."

Flattered, the fifty-four-year-old general accepted the command at once, but with a stipulation. He wanted the President's assurance that once he gave his word to an Indian chief, no desk general in Washington would be allowed to make him a liar. Pierce promised he would do his best to see that this did not happen. But he cautiously reminded Harney that he was being sent to suppress Indians, not adopt them.

"Perhaps if we adopted them," Harney replied boldly, "we might not have to suppress them so often!"

This view received unexpected support that year from Indian Commissioner George Manypenny, who warned Congress, "By alternate persuasion and force, some of these tribes have been removed, step by step, from mountains to valley, and from river to plain, until they have been pushed half-way across the continent. They can go no further. On the ground they now occupy, the crisis must be met, and their future determined."

In the spring of 1855, Harney commanded four companies of the 6th Dragoons and a company of mounted artillery, at Fort Leavenworth, Kansas. Everyone knew that Indian warfare was imminent. The only question was how widespread it would be. The tribes had reached the limit of their endurance of the white man's violations of treaties guaranteeing them the western lands "as long as the rivers shall run and the grass shall grow." They were mad about other outrages, too.

"Abducting Indian children has become quite a common practice," reported one California newspaper on October 2, 1854. "Nearly all of the children belonging to some Indian tribes in the northern part of the State have been stolen. They are taken to the southern part of the State and there sold."

Goldseekers, greedy for Indian mining lands, organized a series of "Indian hunts" and tried to starve out tribes by seizing their food supply of acorns and seeds to use as hog fodder.

Many Indian treaties containing white America's promises to the red man, marked "confidential" by the Senate, remained conveniently "lost" in Senate archives for fully half a century, until searched for and found in 1905.

War with the Sioux broke out when a group of California-bound goldseekers left a sick cow with a peaceful Bois Brule tribe, who were supposed to care for it until it was well, then send it with the next wagon train.

Shortly thereafter, an Oglala Sioux chief visited Chief Black Beaver, who was deeply embarrassed because the white pioneers' depredations of the Bois Brule hunting grounds had left him with insufficient food to prepare a feast for his visitors, as Sioux custom required. The Oglala chief mentioned that he had seen a "white buffalo" on the prairie. Black Beaver explained that it belonged to the white man, whose cattle the Bois Brules never disturbed.

"We do not fear the white man," replied the Oglala. He and his warriors thereupon went on a "hunt" and brought back the white buffalo. The feast was held.

A worried Black Beaver sent word of this development to the emigrant who had owned the cow. The pioneer angrily sent a bill for it to the commanding officer of Fort Laramie. The latter paid it, then sent a lieutenant named Grattan and a force of thirty soldiers to the Bois Brule village to demand the surrender of the Oglala warrior who had killed the cow.

"It is against the Indian custom for a chief to give up a guest to his enemies," Black Beaver protested. "It is true that he has behaved badly. But I cannot deliver him. If you insist upon taking him, he is in that lodge."

"No," said Lieutenant Grattan. "My orders are that you must turn him over to me. I'll give you just five minutes."

Black Beaver shook his head. "I cannot. I would rather be killed by you, Lieutenant, than by my own people for violating the rules of Sioux hospitality."

The cavalryman took out his watch and grimly counted off five minutes. Then he wheeled back toward his troops. "Fire!" he shouted.

Black Beaver dropped with twelve bullets in his body.

The village fell into an uproar. Outraged Bois Brules and Oglalas raced for their weapons. The soldiers opened a scattered fire. Bullets flew back at them in a deadly cross-fire from behind tepees and lodge poles.

In short order, all thirty white troops were killed.

Bugles blew frantically at Fort Laramie. No attempt was made to learn the reason for the massacre. The cry arose: "The only good Injun is a dead Injun!" The cavalry galloped to attack Sioux villages. In short order three hundred Indians were slain, two hundred twenty-five of them women and children. Hacking and cutting up victims' bodies in imitation of the more savage Indian tribes, the soldiers took over one hundred scalps. Some captured Indians were tortured by fire.

The entire Sioux nation rose and went on the warpath.

Daubing war paint on their bronzed skins, they put eagle feathers in their hair and shook their shields four times toward the Indian gods in the sky. They were joined by the Bois Brules, a tribe normally not given to warfare.

General Harney was rushed to Fort Leavenworth, where he led out four companies of dragoons, a portion of the 6th Infantry and a company of mounted artillery. Crossing the North Platte, he made an encampment on high ground known as Ash Hollow. It was a desperately small force to send against the whole Sioux nation and the Bois Brules. But Harney was promised that reinforcements would follow swiftly.

When additional columns rode out of the fort a week or so later, they were led by General Edwin Sumner, the same Bostonian whom Scott had once tried to put over Harney, insisting that the major was a "much safer and more efficient commander" than the colonel.

The deeper Sumner penetrated into Indian country, the more nervous he became. War drums throbbed constantly from the surrounding hills. As the Sioux ghost-danced in the moonlight, he listened tensely to the terrifying *hum-hum-hum* of scalp chants swell in crescendo to a climax of blood-curdling whoops and screams. Convinced that the Sioux were about to encircle and destroy his forces, he panicked and ordered a hasty retreat back to Fort Leavenworth.

There he and his men remained for the winter, leaving Harney to fight the whole Sioux nation with a single regiment. Convinced that Harney was already dead or soon would be, Sumner intended to plead an inability to find his force.

Harney, waiting in vain for Sumner at Ash Hollow, learned about his defection. Infuriated, Harney dispatched a scout with a message for Washington, denouncing Sumner for cowardice and desertion and demanding he be court-martialed. Scott's face darkened when he read it. But his anger was directed at Harney, not at Sumner, one of his favorites. Considering the message more Harney fireworks, he tossed it disdainfully into the waste basket.

Meanwhile, angry young braves of the Bois Brules were demanding vengeance for the murder of Black Beaver and the massacres in the Sioux villages. To appease them, Chief Little Thunder, new leader of the tribe, consented to one attack on a wagon train. Twenty emigrants, including women and children, were killed, and the mails were robbed. Two women were found with dozens of arrows in their bodies, young warriors apparently having raced past on ponies using them for target practice.

When news of this massacre reached General Harney as he rode toward the Sioux country, his face tightened in anger.

Little Thunder would have to be taught a lesson. Harney was willing to overlook a great deal that an Indian did for food for himself and his family. And certainly the idiot lieutenant who killed Black Beaver deserved little sympathy. But killing innocent white women and children was another story. He knew nothing of the killing of Indian women and children in their villages by the troops from Fort Laramie.

His scouts brought him word that the Bois Brules were encamped at Blue Water Creek, a short distance from the North Platte. Harney signaled a change of direction to the guidon. The regimental column swung north toward the river.

An imposing figure in his new field service uniform of loose blue tunic with breeches in lighter blue striped with white, Harney's approach on the proudly trotting white Buncombe did not go unnoticed. Smoke signals sped the news ahead to Little Thunder. The general leading the Army troops against him was none other than Man-who-runs-like-the-Deer.

That afternoon, at the end of a long dusty march, Harney bivouacked his troops beside the Blue Water Creek about twenty miles south of the Bois Brule encampment.

To refresh his hot, weary men and get them in fighting trim for battle, he ordered a regimental swim, which he joined himself.

Then he sharpened their marksmanship with a wild turkey shoot that set sixty-three fowl roasting over open fires that evening. No one enjoyed these unique battle preparations more than Harney himself, who brought down three fowl with bullets carefully placed so as not to tear the game into shreds.

He slept soundly that night in a new buffalo-skin sleeping bag he had fashioned for himself for cold prairie nights. Their tents were pitched under a fringe of good-sized cottonwood trees lining the river bank. Shortly after midnight, Harney woke up suddenly. Buncombe, tethered as usual right outside his tent, was snorting and stamping. Harney knew that Indians were approaching in the distance.

Buncombe was never wrong. Dressing swiftly, he buckled on his sword and told the sentry to rouse the troops. Soon afterward, two pickets rode in to report the approach of three horsemen from the north. Harney lit a lantern, hung it on his tentpole, and waited for his midnight visitors.

The lead horseman, a half-breed trader named Vasquez, carried a white flag. He was followed by two rifle-carrying Bois Brule braves in war paint.

Vasquez said that the reputation of General Man-who-runs-like-the-Deer was known among the Sioux chiefs, who respected him as a soldier to be dreaded in battle. But they also knew him as a friend of the Indian. Little Thunder wanted Harney to understand that he was ready either to fight or to shake hands. Lighting a cigar, Harney replied that he would not shake a hand that shed the blood of women and children. Little Thunder must either give up the hotheads responsible for the raid on the wagon train or prepare to fight.

The truce party rode off. Several hours later sounds of war dances came floating from behind sandstone bluffs that loomed red and ominous to the northeast. Harney decided not to wait. Shortly before dawn, he led his mounted infantry out for a frontal assault on Little Thunder's camp. He sent the cavalry in a circular sweep to the rear of the Bois Brules' position to cut off their retreat.

Galloping at the head of his columns with a Model 1855 pistol carbine in his hand, he saw in the distance that the Bois Brules were hastily striking their painted tepees and retreating up the Blue Water. Suddenly Little Thunder himself, carrying a flag of truce, came riding toward him with an escort of braves. Harney held up his hand.

His men reined their mounts to an abrupt halt.

Trotting up to the American general on a handsome calico pony, Little Thunder made a signal of greeting and held out his hand. He could not surrender the guilty Indians, he pleaded, because they were beyond his control. Harney refused his hand. If Little Thunder could not control the tribe's hotheads, then the cavalry would have to punish them for him. Harney gave him time to return and talk to his people.

The disconsolate Bois Brule chief returned with his escort to the Sioux warriors watching from across the plain. Harney waited. After a while he heard loud war whoops and saw the Indians begin to wheel into battle formations.

He nodded. The regimental bugler blared a charge.

The infantry, mounted on sturdy western mustangs, sorrels, blacks, bays, and grays, galloped toward the Sioux riding against them in a headlong attack. Troop horse crashed into Indian pony. Rifles flamed on both sides.

Indians who had no chance to reload resorted to knives, tomahawks, feathered lances, and arrows. Soldiers wrestled with Indians in fierce hand-to-hand combat on horseback. Sometimes they fought galloping side by side. Knives flashed, mirroring the pale sunlight. War clubs and tomahawks made sickening noises as they slashed through flesh and bone. Indians fell to withering rifle fire. Ponies crashed to earth, spilling riders and colliding with others.

Fighting furiously along with his men, Harney saw a brave racing across his flank hurl a lance at his head. He instinctively flung up his pistol carbine like a stave. The spearhead clashed against it at throat level, clattering off at an angle. Harney flung up the pistol and fired. But at the same moment, his attacker slipped out of the saddle to one side of his pony, riding the surcingle as he scythed his knife against the legs of troop horses.

The plains were filled with the smell of sweating men, horses, and cordite as they fought desperately in the choking dust and smoke swirling up in the raw morning sunlight. Although Little Thunder's forces far outnumbered Harney's regiment, he was so badly out-generaled by the infantry commander that his casualties were seven or eight times as great as those of the mounted troops.

Slowly but surely Harney's skilful generalship swept the Sioux back into a ravine from which the only escape was a narrow pass. Little Thunder tried to lead his forces in a breakout northwest of the Blue Water. But Harney had anticipated that development. His reserves of hard-riding cavalry now charged out at the Sioux from the north, forcing them to turn and race desperately toward the narrow gap that jammed them up like sheep in a shearing pen.

Bois Brule women and children, who had taken refuge in caves under nearby bluffs, grew alarmed at the rout of their warriors. To avoid being left behind and taken prisoner, they rushed out to the ravine to join the turbulent exodus.

Mounted infantry and cavalry raced jubilantly in pursuit of the trapped Sioux. Suddenly the regimental bugler blew a call to halt and cease fire. Stunned and incredulous, the troops reined their mounts and stopped shooting.

A perspiring major galloped up to Harney, his face dark with perplexed frustration. Why were they stopping? The Sioux were cornered—now was the chance to wipe them out!

Broken Treaties and War Drums

11

Harney lit a cigar as he watched the massed Sioux jamming frantically two and three at a time through the bottleneck boulders of the narrow ravine. He did not kill women and children, he told the major acidly, even if some Indian hotbloods did. It was not only a barbaric policy; it was senseless. Tomorrow the Indians would kill more white women and children in revenge. Was this the way to teach them civilized behavior?

The major protested that it was their duty to win the war with the Sioux at all costs. Harney replied that the Bois Brules knew they had been defeated. Showing them mercy now would be more likely to induce them to sue for peace. That meant not only fewer dead Indians, but also fewer dead soldiers and pioneers. The cavalry's job was to keep the peace—not kill Indians or be killed by them.

Harney's estimate of Indian reaction to his humane gesture proved accurate. Little Thunder called a council of Sioux chiefs, persuading them not to fight Man-who-runs-like-the-Deer, who had once more proved that his heart was warm and generous toward the red man. The chiefs sent Harney word that for the time being they would raise no further hand against the white man or his wagon trains, and that all but the Blackfeet were willing to come to a peace parley.

Harney invited them to meet him in the spring at Fort Pierre, South Dakota, his new headquarters. Then he led his forces there as the first snows fell across the vast plains.

On March 1, 1856, all the chiefs of the Sioux nation, including Little Thunder, arrived at Fort Pierre for a five-day council. An impressive array of Indian leaders in long war bonnets, horned headdresses, and buckskin shirts gathered outside the fort walls. Harney emerged to join them, squatting with them on logs as the parley began.

He outlined the Great White Father's demands upon the Sioux. They must give up for punishment the Oglala who had killed the emigrants' cow, but especially the Bois Brules who had killed women and children in the wagon train. All cattle and other property taken in this raid also had to be returned. When the Sioux had done these things, Harney promised, they would receive government credit at the nearest military post, where they could buy the goods they needed.

"And if the white traders behave badly or try to cheat the Sioux," he vowed, "I will throw them out of the country!"

Pleased, the Sioux chiefs nodded.

"I wish to shake hands with you and hold your hands hard," replied Little Thunder. "You have here as prisoners many men, women and children who were in my lodge, and I see they are alive and well. I am glad. When you called me to this council the snow was very bad, but I came because I knew that we could trust you, and that you would give back my people. You have asked us for certain signs of friendship. I will do my best to give them. If I can I will bring in those Indians who have caused the trouble between our people. If I cannot do so, believe that it will not be my fault."

Harney replied, "I am sorry that yours was the first band of Sioux we met, Little Thunder, and so it fell hard upon them. I know there are many good men among your people, but also some bad ones, as with all nations, including my own. But only Sioux chiefs know who their bad people are, and these trouble-makers must be separated from the tribes and delivered to us. I know that all the principal chiefs here today wish to be at peace with us, as we do with them. To prove our own goodwill, Little Thunder may take back all his people whom we have been holding prisoner."

The faces of the Sioux chiefs remained expressionless, but their eyes gave away their feelings for him.

The chief of the Yancton Sioux spoke next. "I traveled all day to get here and did not eat or sleep, and the next day and night I did the same. I am not afraid to lose my life. Starvation is worse. My people have been so hungry that when we saw the white man's cattle, we could not help but slaughter and eat them. Only that kept us alive. No matter how honest a man is, he will take what he must to keep himself and his family from starving."

"That does not make it right," Harney said. "But I understand and cannot be angry in my heart."

"I will not beg you for our lives," went on the Yancton

chief, "although we Sioux are frightened by your riches and your uniforms and your cannons. You ask us to restore the white man's cattle. But I cannot make them from the ground. If this answer displeases you, then you may take my body and sell me, or do whatever you please."

Chief Man-that-is-struck-by-the-Rhee complained hotly, "Many traders weaken our authority by giving out medals, and appointing chiefs who agree to do as they say. Indian agents do the same. When an agent comes here he is poor, but he soon gets rich. After he gets rich he goes away and another poor one comes. There are many thieves among the white men."

"It is true," Harney admitted. "But there are also thieves among the red men. For our part, I give you the word of Man-who-runs-like-the-Deer that the only Sioux chiefs who will be recognized by the Great White Father or myself will be those chosen by the Sioux people themselves. And it is my hope that soon all clans will unite in one great, independent Sioux nation, with your own Sioux government and your own Sioux police force."

Little Thunder looked entranced for a moment, then shook his head. "The Great White Father would never permit such a thing. He would be afraid of a united Sioux nation."

"I will try to convince him," Harney persisted earnestly, "that it would be better than all the trouble caused by attacks upon our wagon trains, or by one Sioux tribe raiding another. I believe each Indian nation should keep its own peace, and be itself responsible for all behavior by their own tribesmen taking place within their own territory."

An intrigued murmur arose among the chiefs. Several shook their war bonnets doubtfully. "Must this be a provision of the treaty?" asked Chief Man-that-is-struck-by-the-Rhee.

Harney thought hard. It was an idea that had been on his mind for some time. Perhaps if he incorporated it into a treaty with the Sioux, the government would be compelled to move in the direction of recognizing the Indian nations in the same way that it recognized foreign nations.

"It must," he replied firmly. "The Sioux are not friends to themselves now. Not until they do what the Great White Father requires of them can I be their friend. But if they agree to these peace terms, they will find me the best friend they ever had. If they refuse—or if they make a treaty and violate it—they will have me on their backs. And they will find me a very hard load to carry!"

After a five-day parley, the Sioux signed the treaty.

Accepting the peace pipe Little Thunder passed to him, General Bill Harney grinned and gave the Sioux chieftain one of his cigars. Then he held out his big horny hand.

"*Now*, Little Thunder, we may shake hands at last!"

Smiling, the two men exchanged handclasps.

Harney forwarded the treaty to Secretary of War Jeff Davis, urging full ratification of all provisions. He asked for a crackdown on traders who were shipping repeating rifles, ammunition, and whiskey into Sioux country, and on Indian agents enriching themselves by cheating red men of their lands and skins. Emphasizing the Sioux complaint that they were compelled to rob cattle because they were starving, he asked the government to provide the tribes with hoes and seed, and agricultural agents to teach them modern farming methods.

"It is not yet too late for us," he wrote Davis, "to requite, in some degree, this unfortunate race for their many sufferings, consequent to the domain of our people on the soil of this continent. These Indians, heretofore proud, stern and unyielding, now ask of us that assistance which all nations have conceded to each other whenever it has been sought. With proper management a new era will dawn upon such of the Indians as yet remain."

Jefferson Davis forwarded his letter, and the treaty, to President Franklin Pierce. The President referred it to Congress for approval. But the Chairman of the Committee on Indian Affairs tossed it aside in total disdain.

"Rubbish!" he told the Committee. "The man is a good soldier, but a political idiot. I never heard a more absurd idea than setting up an Indian government with its own police force. If we listened to Harney, every white man west of the Mississippi would be scalped within two years!"

The treaty went into a desk drawer and stayed there.

Many years later, Indian expert Clark Wissler, Dean of the Scientific Staff, American Museum of Natural History, observed, "Harney seems to have been a man of vision as well as sense. He conceived a plan to organize a native police force and set up a tribal government under the direction of the United States. There is every reason to believe that the plan would have worked and changed Teton history for the better, but this was not to be. Where Indians are concerned, always expect the worst! No one in Washington would even consider the plan."

The Sioux soon realized that the voice of the one white man they trusted carried no real power in the councils of his own government. The frontier reverted to its previous turbulent state. The Nebraska Trail became carpeted in blood under an angry new Sioux leader, Red Cloud. Sioux kinsmen of Black Beaver and Little Thunder sent bitter challenges to Harney at Fort Pierre to meet them in battle.

Disgusted at being sold out once more, the veteran peacemaker bitterly prepared to take the only course now left to him—a new expedition against the disillusioned Sioux who had returned to the warpath.

But fresh orders suddenly came through in September 1856, ordering him instead to trouble-shoot another hot spot—his old campaign grounds in the Everglades. Incredibly, the government was once again having its hands full with the indomitable Seminoles. Billy Bowlegs, last of the Seminole chiefs and a shrewd warrior, had returned to the warpath.

Harney was baffled. He knew Chief Billy well from his previous Florida campaigns. When he had left the Everglades, the Seminole chief had retired to the Big Cypress Swamp to live peacefully off a little garden and banana patch. Billy Bowlegs was not an Indian to start trouble. Harney soon discovered what had infuriated him into fresh revolt.

In December 1855, a party of Army surveyors had discovered Billy's retreat. They had torn up his garden and whacked down his banana plants maliciously—"just to see how old Billy would cut up." When he had gone to their camp to protest, they had pushed him around contemptuously, laughing at his rage. That night Billy had called out the remainder of the Seminole nation. Indian attacks on the surveyors' camp had seriously wounded several officers and men.

During the subsequent two years there were raiding parties by both sides, with many whites and Indians killed and great property damage. By the time Harney reached the Everglades in September 1856, the Billy Bowlegs War was dragging into its eighth discouraging month. Harney felt dispirited by the repetitious stupidity of it all. Tired of persecuting Seminoles who only wanted to be left in peace, he led a few perfunctory chases after Billy in the Big Cypress Swamp. But his heart clearly wasn't in them.

"Mr. Secretary," he wrote urgently to Jeff Davis, "if I give my solemn word to the Seminoles *this* time that we will keep a peace treaty—provided I can get Billy Bowlegs to sign one—can I be *absolutely* certain that Washington won't make a liar out of me again?"

"You have my word," Jeff Davis promised him.

Harney sent for Billy Bowlegs. The Seminole chief did not hesitate to come to his camp, alone and unarmed. Billy knew that the Man-who-runs-like-the-Deer would never himself violate the spirit of a truce. The two men shook hands.

Harney told Billy he was sick and tired of having to "push around" his Indian brothers and that he had a new idea. He would *buy* peace from Billy. Was that fair enough? Let Billy name his price for stopping the war and getting his people to leave for the homes the government had built for the Seminoles on the Upper Arkansas.

Chief Billy Bowlegs's deep eyes bored into his. Would

the Great White Father support his word? Harney replied that he had the promise of the Secretary of War, a good friend and a man to be trusted. The Seminole chief reflected a moment. Then he extended his hand firmly and announced that the Seminole War was over.

The government paid $6,500 to Billy Bowlegs, $1,000 to each of his subchiefs, $500 for each Seminole warrior, and $100 for each woman and child, on condition they agree to emigrate at government expense. From the point of view of the Treasury, it was a great bargain, compared to what the expensive Second Seminole War had cost the government.

Only 150 Seminoles—the last stubborn remnants of a great Indian nation—chose to remain in the swamps, undefeated to the last. The Florida trouble was finally ended.

In May 1857, Harney was ordered to Kansas to keep the peace between warring pro- and antislave factions. The battle between New England abolitionist squatters and "border ruffians" from Missouri had been growing hotter since Kansas' admission into the Union the previous year. Both sides sought to win the election scheduled for October 5, 1857, to determine whether Kansas would be a free state or a slave state.

If slavery won there, it would control the whole Union by tipping power to the South. Abolitionists counted hopefully on Harney's well-known sympathy for the underdog. He couldn't be for the Indian and against the Negro. They told him they relied on him to prevent the "Missouri ruffians" from stealing the election at gunpoint.

His sympathies, he made it clear, had nothing to do

with the struggle in Kansas. President Buchanan had sent him there to keep law and order and prevent bloodshed by either side. That was exactly what he intended to do, nothing more nor less. Whether Kansas chose to vote slave or free was entirely up to the Kansans themselves.

He maintained a strict neutrality.

While in garrison one day he happened to wander into the quarters of one company while its first sergeant, who was ill, was replaced in calling the roll by an old sergeant whom Harney recognized as none other than Koconski, who had served under him in so many Indian campaigns.

Koconski recognized him at the same time. In his confusion, the old soldier began calling off a number of names of men to which no one in the ranks responded. His company commander, still Captain Newton, was embarrassed in General Harney's presence. He upbraided Koconski angrily for calling out names of men who were not on the company roster.

Harney interrupted the tirade. In a low voice he explained that he recognized the names. They were of men in his company during the Second Seminole War, all killed and buried in Florida twenty-two years earlier. Captain Newton's face went gray.

"Don't let that man do any more duty," Harney added quietly. "The poor devil has soldiered long enough."

Then he turned abruptly and left the area.

In April 1858, with Kansas voted safely into the ranks of the free states, Harney was ordered to command an expedition to Utah. The Indians had attacked a wagon train bound for California, killing one hundred twenty emigrants, at Mountain Meadows. They had been incited by the Mormons, who considered themselves at war with the United States because of their political persecution.

Harney's orders were to seize and arrest Brigham Young and his twelve apostles. At the head of three thousand troops and over a thousand supply wagons, he pushed west along roads that were rivers of mud when wet, beaten into deep ruts when dry. Teams bogged down, and sometimes three and four other teams had to be put in harness to get them out of the mire.

Before Harney could reach Salt Lake City, however, Washington came to a political understanding with Brigham Young, who was, after all, a white, not Indian, chieftain. Harney was ordered instead to Fort Vancouver to replace a general named Clarke, who had been unable to check Indians on the warpath in the Washington and Oregon territories.

When General Clarke received the news that Harney was on his way, he hastily summoned a council of Flat Head, Spokane, Coeur d'Alene, Nez Perce, and Walla Walla chiefs.

"You have refused my peace terms," Clarke told them, "but I have news that may make you change your minds. The great white war chief, General Harney, whose fame as an Indian-fighter is well-known to all tribes, is on his way to take command here. His orders are to wage a great war upon you, after which terms for peace will be much more severe!"

Chief No Horns On His Head, a proud Nez Perce with a ring through his nose and long black hair that flowed over his painted shirt, replied, "The Man-who-runs-like-the-Deer will not seek to destroy us. He knows that we have never yet killed a white man nor broken a promise. Can our white brothers say this? We know, too, that Man-who-runs-like-the-Deer is a true friend of the Indian, not our enemy."

"All that you say is true," Clarke admitted. "But this time General Harney has no choice. His orders strictly forbid him to make any overtures of friendship to any Indian nation until he has first punished those tribes that continue to be hostile toward the Government."

The chiefs deliberated among themselves.

Finally a Walla Walla chief spoke up. "It shall be as you say, then. We will sign a treaty of friendship if you will tell Man-who-runs-like-the-Deer that his Indian brothers do not wish to fight him, but desire only his hand."

So by nothing more than the sheer weight of his fame, prestige and goodwill among the red men of America, General Bill Harney ended an Indian war without even knowing it.

Clash in the Northwest

No one was more astonished and pleased at this development than Harney himself. When he arrived at Fort Vancouver, the tribes of the northwest lived up to their treaty, surrendering into Harney's hands those Indians who had been guilty of hostile acts against white settlements.

So instead of fighting another pointless Indian war, the silver-haired general busied himself directing surveys of passable routes for emigrants from Salt Lake City through the Oregon Territory to the coast. He set up frontier posts to protect them from hostile outbreaks as they moved through the Indian Territory and to protect the Indians from mistreatment at the hands of unscrupulous white men.

Surveying the South Dakota frontier to make official maps, government engineers escorted by General George Custer and his troops found a jagged peak that towered above all others on a limestone plateau of the Red Valley. In a symbolic tribute, Custer's men fired off a salute as the landmark was named Harney's Peak, which name it bears today. Oregon also honored him by naming its largest county after him, bearing within it the town of Harney, Harney Valley, and Harney Lake. Oregonians had good reason to remember him.

To help protect the Indians of the northwest and to keep them at peace, Harney asked the War Department to appoint Father P. J. De Smet, a Jesuit missionary, as an Army chaplain under his command. Like himself, De Smet was greatly admired and respected by the Flat Heads and other tribes of the Columbia River. He was a former Belgian nobleman who had lived with Indians from Chile to Alaska.

He suffered their privations, comforted them, shared their roots and berries, or dogs and ponies when there was nothing else to eat. He never betrayed an Indian trust to the white man. Known as Black Gown, he was a welcome guest in every Indian lodge along the west coast of both Americas, and could speak a dozen Indian languages and dialects. A classical scholar, he had deep respect for, and understanding of, Indian culture, considering it in many ways superior to the culture of the white man.

Long before white men discovered gold in the Black Hills, some Indian girls brought Father De Smet a heavy gold nugget the size of a quail's egg that they had found in a streambed, asking him what it was. He explained in the Sioux dialect that it was the white man's money and that the white man loved nothing in the world so much. He would risk his life for it, kill for it, make war for it. He must never hear that they had found the shining stone; they must never tell where or how they got it. If they did, the white man would come like the grasshopper clouds to take their beautiful country away from them. The secret was kept.

De Smet was one of Bill Harney's trump cards in keeping the northwest peaceful. He sent the missionary from tribe to tribe as his goodwill ambassador and personal trouble-shooter, seeing to it that the terms of the treaty were carried out and giving ear to Indian grievances.

On one occasion a vindictive Indian agent arrested and imprisoned some former chiefs who had once been powerful, but had now fallen upon evil days. De Smet found them poverty-stricken, sick, and in one case half-blind. He urged Harney to come to their rescue. Harney did so at once, ordering their immediate release from arrest and commanding the chagrined Indian agent to provide them with food, clothing, and medicine.

Harney always looked forward to De Smet's return from his trips through Indian territory, finding the missionary one of the most stimulating, intelligent, and wholly admirable white men in the west. De Smet, in turn, respected Harney as a rare military specimen—an American general with a genuine conscience about Indians.

If his dream of an independent Indian government ever did come true, De Smet once teased him, it would probably ask him to serve as its ambassador to the United States. Harney replied dryly that he would accept if De Smet would agree to go along and pacify the most hostile tribe in America for him—the United States Congress.

In December 1858, now fifty-eight years old and grown more crotchety with the years, Bill Harney found himself ironically cast in a reversal of the firebrand role he had played all his life—that of a military maverick rebelling against his superior officers. He began to have insubordination trouble of his own and was no less irked by it than Generals Scott, Macomb, and Wool had been by his own brashness as a junior officer.

No martinet, Harney was nevertheless angered by the lax discipline and insolence of the young officers at Fort Vancouver, most of them spoiled scions pushed into a military career by wealthy families. When he arrived at the fort, he found them running it as a kind of private social club, with the enlisted men being used as flunkeys.

He promptly instituted drills and parades to make the junior officers understand that the old privileged days under General Clarke were gone. Resenting him, they sought every opportunity for revenge by harassing him.

When First Lieutenant Joshua W. Sill, a young ordnance officer, arrived at Fort Vancouver to supervise building an arsenal, the junior officers encouraged him to claim special pay allowances due a senior ordnance officer. He was "senior," they convinced him, because he was the only one. Amused but irked, Harney denied the application. The young officers prodded Sill into writing an openly insolent protest.

Now genuinely angered, Harney ordered his arrest to teach him a lesson. But not really wanting to punish him, Harney offered to drop the charges if Sill would reword his protest with the required military courtesy. The other young officers urged him to refuse and Sill did.

Harney promptly had him court-martialed.

With quarters at Fort Vancouver primitive and cramped, Harney decided to build a cabin in the woods nearby for himself and his adjutant, a captain named Pleasonton. Offering leaves of absence to mechanics and laborers in his regiment who wanted to volunteer for the job, he paid them civilian wages out of his own pocket. He worked alongside them daily with axe, hatchet, hammer, and saw. The volunteers enjoyed the break from Army routine and were delighted to have a naked-to-the-waist general as a fellow builder.

The fort's young officers saw their chance to get back at Harney. They egged on a new artillery officer who had arrived only three weeks before, First Lieutenant Henry V. De Hart, to write a snide and insolent protest to Harney's adjutant about the men's leaves of absence.

Captain Pleasonton sent it back to De Hart to be reworded in polite military language. De Hart's next effort was even more insolent. Back it came again. De Hart submitted a third, flagrantly offensive version. Pleasonton firmly rejected it a third time. De Hart finally burst into the adjutant's office and delivered an angry tirade.

Pleasonton dismissed him as a pest. De Hart shrieked that he had been insulted. "Not only that, Captain," he yelled shrilly, "but I'm holding you personally responsible for the illegal acts of General Harney!"

The silver-haired general promptly came to the aid of his adjutant, ordering De Hart's arrest. Charges were submitted to the War Department and a court-martial requested. But suddenly Bill Harney's old enemy, Army Chief of Staff Winfield Scott, decided to pay off some ancient scores. He wrote Harney that the War Department would not entertain his charges and coldly requested De Hart's release.

The veteran Indian fighter was stunned. He appealed to Secretary of War John B. Floyd over Scott's head. If he released De Hart, it would be impossible for him to maintain discipline afterward. The officers under him would know he was powerless to curb insubordination. He asked that the matter be brought to the attention of President James Buchanan and that Scott be ruled out of order as "a weak or envious commander-in-chief having purposes of his own detrimental to the honor and dignity of the service."

Instead of sending his protest to the President, Floyd showed it to Scott. He was well within his rights to do this because Harney, in violating the chain of command, was just as guilty of a breach of military etiquette as De Hart.

Scott, infuriated, attacked Harney as a vengeance-mad roughneck full of "besotted notions"—an unfair insinuation, since Harney was no hard drinker. It was not safe, Scott insisted, to leave the Oregon Department in the hands of a general so ruled by "ignorance, passion and caprice."

Supporting his chief of staff, Floyd ordered De Hart released and rebuked Harney for going over Scott's head. But Floyd turned a conveniently deaf ear to Scott's wrathful insistence that Harney be removed from his command.

During the summer of 1859, immigration to the new state of Oregon and to the Washington Territory began to swell from a trickle to a flood, along the new road surveyed and built under Harney's direction and protection. He provided the wagon trains with troop escorts against possible attack by one of the few renegade Indian bands. For the most part, however, the territory was relatively quiet thanks to his prestige among the Indians, reinforced by Father De Smet's indefatigable travels as his personal representative.

During this same year, Harney became the keystone of a touchy situation that almost plunged the United States into a third war with Great Britain. The island of San Juan in Puget Sound was under control of the British Hudson Bay Company. Whether the island was properly English or American territory remained in dispute. The island's English and American settlers clashed constantly.

The Americans were terrorized by a band of nomadic Indian headhunters called the Stickens, who were given carte blanche for their raids by the Hudson Bay Company, as long as British citizens weren't touched. A war situation developed when one American settler complained to the company that a British settler's pig was damaging his crops and asked that it be penned. His request was ignored. He shot the pig, then offered to pay the company twice its value.

This trivial incident was the spark that touched off the powder keg of war preparations. The next day a British man-of-war pulled into the island to arrest the American pig-killer and take him to Victoria to stand trial. Seizing his rifle, he growled that they'd have to kill him first. A Hudson Bay Company representative coldly suggested that the British might not have to go to this trouble. They could suggest to their headhunting friends the Stickens that *all* American trespassers on the island were no longer welcome.

The outraged Americans appealed for help to General Harney at Fort Vancouver. He promptly sailed to the island himself to investigate the trouble. Convinced that the complaint of these white settlers was justified, Harney ordered a company of the 9th Infantry under a captain named Pickett to garrison San Juan Island. He placed additional troops on the steamer *Massachusetts*, and kept them cruising in Puget Sound as a reserve force. Pickett was given two orders—to keep the Indian headhunters off San Juan and to fight any attempt by the British to arrest American citizens.

When news of what Harney had done reached the White House, President Buchanan, a vacillating man overwhelmed by the stormy passions of the time, was greatly upset. Here the government was trying to straighten out its boundary disputes with Great Britain and Harney had charged in to take military possession of one of the disputed islands!

But Secretary of War Floyd wondered if the British might not be getting ready to grab it themselves. He advised the President to sit tight and to see what happened. Harney was instructed to be sure the British understood United States forces were on the island only to protect American citizens from the Stickens and that their presence was not to be construed as a military seizure or occupation.

Harney made this explanation in a letter to the head agent of the Hudson Bay Company. The latter replied with a frosty note to Captain Pickett on the island, giving him and his troops two days to clear out. To make this message perfectly clear, His Majesty's thirty-gun frigate, the *Tribune*, pulled off just offshore of the island, broadside to the camp of the 9th Infantry company.

Pickett sent an urgent message to Harney for help. Dispatching four more companies to the island, Harney asked the Navy to send a squadron of available warships to Puget Sound. Four additional British men-of-war sailed down in an ominous convoy from Vancouver. War seemed inevitable.

Harney received a message from British Governor James of Vancouver, demanding that he pull his military forces out of San Juan Island or suffer the consequences. He replied that every American soldier on the island would stay put until he received orders from his government to take them off.

Alarmed by the dangerous situation, Buchanan rushed General Scott to Oregon, urging him to do whatever was necessary to prevent war. Scott proved an excellent diplomat and won a peaceful compromise of the dispute. Ultimately, the British yielded San Juan Island, as well as the neighboring archipelago, to the United States.

"Harney may be good at making peace with the Indian nations," Scott sniffed to President Buchanan upon his return to Washington, "but he is certainly no diplomat when it is necessary to deal with *real* nations!"

Harney turned his attention to matters closer to his heart—Indian grievances. He pressured the Bureau of Indian Affairs to relieve their growing hardships as the result of spreading white settlements in Oregon and Washington. His complaints on their behalf found their way into the 1859 report of the United States Commissioner of Indian Affairs, who told Congress that year:

"We have substantially taken possession of the Western Territories and deprived the Indians of their accustomed means of support. Numbers of them are compelled to sustain life by using for food reptiles, insects, grass, seeds and roots. They have at times been compelled to either steal or starve. Many of the numerous depredations have doubtless been committed by them in consequence of their destitute and desperate condition." But Congress, engrossed in the growing conflict between slave and free states, paid no attention.

In July 1860, Harney was ordered to St. Louis to take command of the Department of the West. He arrived in St. Louis a week after the Pony Express had begun service from St. Joseph to California. Warmly embraced by his son John, who was now living in their old home, he was given some worrisome news. John had just received a letter from his sister Anna, who was now married to a French naval officer named Viscount de Thury, that Mary had fallen very ill in Paris. She was being cared for by the Harneys' other daughter, Eliza, whose husband, Count De Noue, was a colonel in the French Army. Deeply worried, Harney left for Washington.

Reproaching himself for having been absent from his family so long, he asked the President if he could be spared long enough for a leave to Paris. Buchanan replied that he was sorry to hear that Harney's wife was not well and of course if he must go to her, he should have his leave. But his request came at a highly dangerous time in the country's affairs. Civil war might explode at any moment, Buchanan warned, and he had few generals he could really rely upon to keep aloof from politics and intrigue. They leaned to one side or the other. Buchanan was a northerner who placed the Union above all else, and he considered Harney a southerner who believed the same. Harney, he said, was desperately needed now in the midwest to keep all factions calm and to deal with them fairly.

Harney cancelled his request for leave.

Buchanan detained him for several weeks, consulting him on military precautions in the event that the dreaded civil war broke out. Harney reported to the President once each morning and again each evening. Buchanan would listen carefully to his strategy for fortifying the southern seaboard, cutting off any rebel states from British aid and securing the ports for landing federal troops.

The President would nod in agreement with Harney's plans in the morning, only to express grave doubts in the evening. The reason for his vacillation was that in between he would also consult Secretary of War John B. Floyd, a Virginian with strong southern sympathies.

Soon after Harney's return to St. Louis to take up command of the Department of the West, he received word from his daughter Eliza that Mary had died and been buried in Paris. For almost a week he was numb with grief and guilt. But his melancholy had to be shaken off in a rush of military preparations as civil war drew nearer.

Pressured by Missouri sympathizers on both sides of the conflict, he had no doubts where his allegiance lay. He still believed what Jackson had taught him long ago—that a soldier owed unswerving loyalty to the Republic. It was this unshakable belief that had compelled him to fight Indian wars, the wisdom and justice of which he strongly doubted, because the government had ordered him to do so. With Tennyson, he believed in the code of professional soldiers: "Theirs not to reason why; theirs but to do and die."

Like Buchanan, he was dismayed at the rapidity with which the Republic he cherished was falling into chaos over the slavery question. Like the President, too, he sought to hold himself aloof from all political intrigues, concentrating on preserving peace, law, and order. He opposed slavery, but he was not willing to see the Republic blown apart over it by hotheads of the north and south.

His refusal to favor the south antagonized many St. Louis officials and influential friends who expected this partiality of him as a Tennessee-born military. man who knew intimately many important southern sympathizers. His refusal to favor the north made him distrusted by abolitionist leaders impatient with compromise.

Harney's old comrades of the Indian and Mexican wars began to emerge as key figures in the brewing explosion. In February 1861, Captain Abe Lincoln became the new President of the United States—four days after another old friend of the Black Hawk days, Lieutenant Jeff Davis, was elected President of the Southern Confederacy.

Then in April his fellow veterans of the Cerro Gordo campaign in the Mexican War took their stand in the new conflict. General T. P. Beauregard attacked Fort Sumter in Charleston Harbor and seized it. Colonel Robert E. Lee resigned his United States Army commission to accept command of the Confederate forces in Virginia.

In that same month Fort Caswell and Fort Johnson in North Carolina were taken by rebel forces, and a Union commander abandoned and burned the United States arsenal at Harper's Ferry, Virginia. Control of federal forts and arsenals was vital to both sides in the full-scale civil war that was now inevitable.

Harney grew deeply concerned about the major arsenal in St. Louis, whose possession could be the key to control of Missouri and the whole Department of the West. He became aware of a power duel between Captain Nathaniel Lyon, who commanded the arsenal, and General D. M. Frost, commander of Camp Jackson. Lyon had organized the Union Party in Missouri, and was working secretly with Congressman Francis P. Blair, Jr. to sweep Missouri into the Union camp.

Harney suspected a counterplot led by pro-secession Governor Claiborne Jackson and General Frost to seize the St. Louis arsenal and win Missouri for the Confederacy. Relaying his suspicions to Lincoln's new Secretary of War, Simon Cameron, he urged that an officer of the highest rank be assigned to the arsenal to oppose General Frost, if the latter should attempt to take it by force or by imposing his authority over that of a mere captain.

On April 23, 1861, Cameron ordered Harney to report to Washington. Harney left at once, prepared to give the new Secretary of War a thorough briefing in the delicate Missouri situation. En route he looked forward to seeing again the other long-legged "pony" with whom he had once spent enjoyable evenings swapping jokes around the campfires of the Illinois wilderness. He wondered whether being President had changed old Abe's priceless sense of humor.

On April 25, the train suddenly stopped at Harper's Ferry. A young Confederate officer flung open the door of the car in which he was riding. Heels clicking smartly, he strode to Harney's seat, hand on his sword hilt.

"General Harney, sir, you are my prisoner!"

The Final Betrayal

13

The sixty-one-year-old grizzled veteran stared at the beardless youth in amazement and contempt. Rising without expression, he swung a vigorous fist that still held its power.

The southerner flew backward, crashing against a seat.

Harney walked toward him calmly. Ignoring his sidearms, he put his gloved hands on his hips and stood in the aisle, legs apart, staring down at the fallen gladiator.

Then he exploded. "Blast your soul—get out of here!"

Several other Confederate officers raced into the car. Saluting deferentially, they explained that he must consider himself their prisoner. They had a whole battalion surrounding the train, sent with the specific mission of intercepting him before he reached Washington.

And so he became the very first prisoner taken by the South in the Civil War. His captors escorted him to Richmond, where he found that leaders of the Confederate cause had gathered. Many were old acquaintances. One was Governor John Letcher of Virginia, a close friend of his old idol General Jackson. Letcher quickly apologized for the clumsy manner in which he had been brought to Virginia's capital.

His arrest at Harper's Ferry had really been a blunder, Letcher told Harney blandly. The officer in charge of the battalion hadn't realized he was simply supposed to offer the general a military escort to Richmond, not take him prisoner. The important thing was that the south needed him. How did he feel about a Confederate command under Lee?

The white-bearded general folded his arms, and his answer was evident in the stiffening of his back. He was a man of his word, he told the governor. He had never once broken his word to the Indians. Forty-four years earlier he had given his word to the United States government, and he certainly didn't intend breaking *that* word now either.

Robert E. Lee was asked to change his mind in a private conference. Typical old soldiers, the two generals exchanged reminiscences of their campaign against Santa Anna.

Then there was an awkward silence.

"General," Harney said pointedly, "I have the greatest respect for you as a man and an officer. But I must admit I am mighty sorry to meet you again in this way."

Lee looked genuinely stricken. "General Harney," he said sadly, "I had no idea of taking any part in this matter. I wanted to stay at Arlington and raise potatoes for my family, but my friends forced me into it."

Another southern general, Joseph E. Johnston, also told Harney plaintively that he was opposed to the rebellion, but all his relatives lived in Virginia. Had he refused to join the southern cause, he would have been a family outcast.

When Harney persisted in his refusal to accept a command with Lee's army, he was permitted to continue his interrupted journey to Washington. Letcher apologized for any inconvenience they had caused him, and hoped they would meet again under less desperate circumstances.

His fame as an Indian-fighter and Mexican war hero was still so vivid in the public mind that news of his impending arrival sent crowds jamming into every station en route for a glimpse of him. With his usual distaste for ovations, he buried himself behind a newspaper. But at one station crowds refused to let the train pull out unless he agreed to stick his head out of the car window. The conductor pleaded with him to oblige so that the train could arrive on schedule.

Sighing, Harney lowered his paper, put his head out the window and even suffered himself to wave. Then the train inched its way through the cheering mobs lining the tracks.

When he arrived in Washington, he received an unpleasant shock. He learned that he had not been summoned by Cameron for consultation. He had been summarily relieved of his command of the Department of the West. There was even more depressing news. An ugly rumor was circulating that he had been a willing prisoner of the State of Virginia, and that he was considering resigning his commission in the Army of the United States to fight beside Robert E. Lee.

Both these blows were the work of the powerful Blair family of Washington. Rich and important, with influence in every department of government, the Blairs had private plans to gain control of the country for their own purposes.

Their source of power in the East was the Lincoln administration. In the west they planned to operate through General John Frémont, the unsuccessful Republican candidate against Buchanan, putting him in control of the Department of the West. To do that they first had to get rid of Harney, whom they knew would not allow himself to be manipulated by either threats or promises.

Lincoln was indebted to the Blairs because he had needed their support as the political power in both Maryland and Missouri, pivotal border states indispensable for his election. Montgomery Blair had been rewarded with the Cabinet post of Postmaster General. A tall, lean man with hard, deepset eyes, carefully weighing every word he spoke, Blair quickly intervened in War Department affairs to carry out the schemes his father and brothers had plotted with him.

The proud boast of the Blairs was, "We make men!" They were also experts at unmaking them. Montgomery Blair applied pressure on Secretary of War Cameron to remove Harney. Cameron at first refused, defending Harney's brilliant record of service to his country, as well as his great value to the Union as a southern general loyal to the north. The head of the Blair clan, Francis P. Blair, publisher of the powerful Washington *Globe*, then stormed into the office of General Scott, insisting that this longtime foe of Harney add his pressure on Cameron to oust him from his vital post.

Scott hesitated. No one could accuse him of being fond of the gruff, trigger-tempered Indian-fighter with whom he had so often clashed bitterly. Yet he had deep respect for Harney as a military man, as well as for his courage and dedication to duty. Harney's removal, Scott knew, would be both a gross injustice and a serious loss to the Union.

At one stroke Winfield Scott made amends for much of the churlish injustice he had visited upon Harney over the years. He flatly refused to bow to Blair family pressure that Harney be sacrificed for their political schemes.

"You are wasting your time!" he told Francis Blair. "I do not like General Harney, but I fully respect him!"

The Blairs, nevertheless, prevailed. Their power was such that they were also later able to force even the resignation of Secretary of the Treasury Salmon Chase, who then angrily accused Lincoln of being a helpless tool in the hands of the unscrupulous Blair family.

Abe Lincoln greeted Harney warmly at a White House reception, and the two men exchanged amused reminiscences over their Black Hawk War days. Then Harney said, "Mr. President, I know how busy you are these days, but if you have a free moment I would appreciate discussing certain matters."

"Certainly, General," Lincoln nodded. "I would hope that perhaps I can explain those matters better to you."

But before that private meeting could take place, a dramatic turn of events took place in St. Louis. On cue from Congressman Francis Blair, Jr., Captain Lyon of the St. Louis arsenal, commanding the 2nd Infantry, marched on Camp Jackson. Charging that General Frost was plotting with the Confederacy to put the camp in their hands and then seize the arsenal, Lyon forced General Frost's surrender and took his forces prisoner. The fat was in the fire.

Frost indignantly wrote to Harney in Washington that Lyon's action was totally illegal and that nothing and no one at Camp Jackson had in any way proposed disloyalty to the Union. The whole state of Missouri had fallen into an uproar. An alarmed Secretary of War Cameron decided that the dangerous controversy called for the cool hand of a man respected by both sides as absolutely impartial.

He quickly reappointed Harney to the command of the Department of the West, ordering him to return to St. Louis at once. Harney conducted a swift and thoroughly impartial investigation. He found that Lyon had told the truth substantially, and that Governor Claiborne Jackson and General Frost had, in fact, been plotting to seize the arsenal and declare Missouri for the Confederacy.

His report to Cameron supported Lyon's seizure of Camp Jackson and reaffirmed Harney's determination to keep Missouri at peace, with protection for its citizens against both Confederate sympathizers and abolitionists.

Even though Harney had vindicated him, Lyon remained committed to the Blair conspiracy to replace Harney with Frémont, in order to capture Missouri for the Union. As a zealous abolitionist personally, Lyon also scorned Harney's neutrality on the slavery question.

Most abolitionists saw an inconsistency in Harney's position. Why should he be much more indignant over the injustices to the red man than to the black? He had never let his uniform prevent him from protesting bitterly to the government against persecution of the tribes. His opposition to the white man's mistreatment of the black man, however, had been kept to a personal level.

Was this distinction the result of his Tennessee birth or his many Southern friends? Or was his fear of the destruction of the Republic so great that his chief concern was not justice for the Negro but preservation of the Union?

His compassion for the Indians as underdogs, and his stern rebuffs to Confederate officials and officers who urged him to join them, would suggest that, like Lincoln, he was sincerely opposed to slavery, but first and foremost anxious to prevent the country he cherished and had served so well from breaking up into two hostile nations.

There is another factor that may have been a consideration in the difference of passion he displayed over the grievances of the red man and the black man. At this time in the history of the country, and for many decades before, there was a constantly swelling chorus of protest over slavery led by the abolitionists. But few voices of outrage were raised to denounce the persecution of the red Americans.

In May 14, 1861, Harney issued a proclamation to the people of Missouri, urging loyalty to the Union and exposing the Confederate plot to seize the state for the south. This act still did not satisfy the militant Republican radicals of Missouri, who considered Harney too mild in his opposition to the state's Confederate sympathizers, whom they wanted jailed.

"Can't you have General Harney sent away from here?" fretted one St. Louis abolitionist in a letter to Postmaster General Montgomery Blair. "If he remains here much longer, we shall be compelled a second time to conquer a peace in Missouri. Can't a division of the Army be made for him, embracing Utah and the Indians?"

This suggestion, although offered as a plan to dispose of

Harney diplomatically, also reflected a strong sentiment by the Union command in Missouri that Harney was needed to organize and lead an Indian army against secessionist forces in the southwest. Because of the opposition of the Blair family, who were determined to concentrate all military power in the west under Frémont, this Indian army was never raised under Harney to fight for the Union.

"If that had been done," General John McNeil wrote after the Civil War, "such was the power of General Harney's name in Arkansas and the Southwest that Missouri would, I am convinced, have been saved from pillage and destruction, and a wedge inserted between the Confederacy and her best source of supplies, that would have materially shortened the war."

Instead, Montgomery Blair pressured Lincoln to give his Congressman brother Francis a commission as a general, with standby orders to relieve Harney of his command. The order would be served when "General" Francis Blair considered the time opportune. Montgomery Blair wrote this news to his brother in St. Louis, along with his estimate of Harney:

"I think it possible that if Harney had about him some resolute, sensible men, he would be right all the time. It is only because he falls into the hands of our opponents that he is dangerous; his intention being good, but his judgment being weak. . . . It is better to mortify him than to endanger the lives of many men, and the position of Missouri, in the present conflict."

Lincoln had serious misgivings about dismissing Harney, but his trust in, and obligation to, Montgomery Blair overcame them. How sorely the matter troubled him is evident in the letter he sent to Francis Blair in St. Louis on May 18, 1861, after much soul-searching agony.

"We have a good deal of anxiety here about St. Louis," he wrote. "I understand an order has gone from the War Department to you, to be delivered or withheld in your discretion, relieving General Harney from his command. I was not quite satisfied with the order when it was made, though on the whole I thought it best to make it; but since then I have become more doubtful of its propriety. I do not write now to countermand it, but to say I wish you would rehold it, unless in your judgment the necessity to the contrary is very urgent."

He added, "There are several reasons for this. We better have him a *friend* than an *enemy*. It will dissatisfy a good many who otherwise would be quiet. More than all, we first relieve him, then restore him; and now if we relieve him again the public will ask, 'Why all this vacillation?' Still, if in your judgment it is *indispensable*, let it be so. Yours very truly, A. Lincoln."

On May 30, 1861, after forty-three years of brilliant service that mirrored American history from 1818 to the Civil War, Brigadier-General William Harney was let out to pasture. Relieved of command, he was granted "leave of absence until further orders"—orders that never came.

The Blair family celebrated their triumph.

But General Winfield Scott, Harney's old enemy, told Montgomery Blair sourly, "I suppose you know that the removal of General Harney, to satisfy your family's ambitions, will probably cost the Government about 100,000 men and $100,000,000 in military equipment. The South will be eternally grateful to you, Mr. Blair!"

The disastrous battle of Bull Run occurred seven weeks after Harney's removal. Three weeks later Union forces under Lyon, now a general, were defeated at Wilson's Creek, Missouri. That same month the Blairs' man, General John C. Frémont, now in command of the Department of the West, proclaimed martial law and declared freedom for the slaves of any white Missourian who took up arms against the north.

The uproar this decree caused was so great that three days later Lincoln was forced to order it modified. Shortly thereafter he fired Frémont for both insubordination and incompetence. "The removal of General Harney," Lincoln said bitterly in a reproach to Montgomery Blair, "was one of the greatest mistakes of my administration!"

Bill Harney was understandably grieved at this final betrayal by the government he had served so faithfully.

"My whole course as commander of the Department of the West," he protested to the adjutant general of the Army in Washington, "has been dictated by a desire to carry out, in good faith, the instructions of my government, regardless of the clamor of the conflicting elements surrounding me, and whose advice and dictation could not be followed without involving the State in blood and the government in the unnecessary expenditure of millions. Under the course I pursued Missouri was secured to the Union . . . a bloodless victory. But those who clamored for blood have not ceased to impugn my motives."

He added with bristling indignation, "During a long life dedicated to my country I have seen some service, and more than once I have held her honor in my hand, and during that time my loyalty, I believe, was never questioned." Declaring his willingness to leave it to posterity's unbiased judgment to decide how loyally he had served his country, he asked for the opportunity for further service "that will testify to the love I bear her."

But the Blair family saw to it that he did not get that opportunity. Saddened by the apparent end of his usefulness to the nation, Bill Harney retired in 1864.

It was small consolation to him that in this same year Abraham Lincoln decided that he had had more than enough of the political machinations of the Blair family. On September 23, the President wrote coolly to Montgomery Blair, "My Dear Sir: You have generously said to me, more than once, that whenever your resignation could be a relief to me, it was at my disposal. The time has come."

But it came too late for justice to be done to General Bill Harney, as it was already too late for justice to be done to the American Indians whose lost cause he had championed.

In 1862 the government, worried about Indians joining the Confederacy, tried to placate them with a long-overdue change of policy. Secretary of the Interior Caleb Smith announced a "radical change in the mode of treatment of Indians." They would henceforth be regarded as "wards" of the government, to be protected against hostile United States Army military authorities who were, even then, attempting to suppress new uprisings of the Plains Indians as the railroads began invading the Indian Territory.

The new Indian wars were highly unpopular with the public, not because of humanitarian sentiments, but because they were so costly. Between 1862 and 1867, wars with just the Sioux, Cheyennes, and Navajos cost the government $100 million. An 1868 estimate of the cost of killing each Indian worked out to a staggering $1,000,000 apiece.

Most Americans of the day agreed with the policy of reclaiming the western lands from the Indians, sweeping the red men out of the way onto reservations where the land was useless for farming, grazing, mining, or settling. But surely, Congressmen rose to protest, there must be some less costly and less troublesome way to do it?

When the Civil War was over Congress appointed an Indian Peace Commission, ordering its members to travel through the west and investigate the main reasons why the tribes were on the warpath and what could be done about it.

The commission was headed by Civil War hero General William Tecumseh Sherman, who immediately asked Bill Harney, as the nation's greatest Indian expert, to serve with him. They swung around the west visiting tribes and listening to Indian grievances. The sixty-five-year-old Indian-fighter had few illusions about the real intentions of Congress in setting up the Indian Peace Commission. But he was determined to make the most of this last chance to convince his government of truths he had vainly been trying to make Washington understand throughout his career as an army man.

The commission accumulated masses of shocking data that indicted the federal government for unfulfilled treaty promises, military ruthlessness, and fraud by Indian agents.

"The records are abundant to show that agents have pocketed the funds appropriated by the Government and driven the Indians to starvation," the commission report stated. The Sioux uprising in Minnesota in 1862 had been just one of many such Indian wars caused by such corruption.

One Cheyenne chief in the Powder River region of Montana listened in cynical silence to the commission's avowal of peaceful intentions. Then he pointed back along the Bozeman Trail to where a new fort was being built.

"You ask my nation to let your people and wagons pass through our hunting grounds to the gold country," he said. "But you build forts all along the trail. We are not fools. If we do not agree to a treaty, you will invade our land anyhow. If we sign a treaty, the forts mean you do not trust us to keep it. This is how it has always been. The Great White Father has a bad conscience about his own word—so he does not trust the Indian to keep his!"

Harney Tells It Like It Is

14

Nomadic tribes everywhere were infuriated over the white man's slaughter of the buffalo. More than the red man's food supply was involved. Buffalo skins made up the Indians' winter clothing, bed, blanket, tepees, moccasins, leggings, shirts, and children's things. Boats were made from the fresh hides stretched over cottonwood hoops. The paunch lining provided water buckets. Sinews yielded thread and bowstrings.

Spoons and bows were made from the horns. The ribs became prairie sleds. Glue came from the hoofs. Buffalo droppings served as fuel. The tail made flyswatters. Hides the Indians didn't need were traded to the white man for arrowheads, vermilion, beads, awls, blankets, cloth, knives, kettles, sugar, coffee, mirrors, and other household goods.

But new Army posts in the west were hiring professional hunters like young "Buffalo Bill" Cody to furnish their garrisons with buffalo meat. Trainloads of Eastern "sportsmen hunted buffalo from train windows, killing or crippling as many as five hundred buffaloes in each herd a train passed.

In its first year of operation, the new Dodge City, Kansas, firm of Rath & Wright alone shipped over 200,000 buffalo hides east. Hide hunters killed 12,500,000 buffalo between 1870 and 1875. "The hell with the Indians," declared professional hide hunter Hank Campbell. "If they want to powwow, we'll let our Sharps do the talking for us." By 1878 the vast southern herd was almost exterminated.

"Protect the buffalo, hell!" General Phil Sheridan, military commander of the southwest, defied conservationists. "The hide hunters have done more to solve the Indian problem than the Army has been able to do in 30 years. Let them kill, skin and sell until the buffalo is exterminated, as it is the only way to bring about a lasting peace and allow civilization to advance!"

And the white man killed, skinned, and sold.

When the last large herd of ten thousand buffalo was wiped out in 1883, Chief Sitting Bull said, "My heart is on the ground. A cold wind blew across the prairie when the last buffalo fell—a death-wind for my people."

In vain did the Indian Peace Commission seek to prevent this tragedy sixteen years earlier. Even before returning to report to Congress, General Sherman issued an order forbidding the invasion of the Sioux country by parties of white men. But the order was simply ignored in the wild rush to the Black Hills as the gold lodes Father De Smet had tried to keep secret were finally discovered.

The white men came, just as the missionary had warned the Sioux, "like the grasshopper clouds to take your beautiful country away from you."

When the Indian Peace Commissioners reported back to Congress, they testified that nine out of ten Indian outbreaks had been provoked by outrages committed by white men. The pattern was invariably the same. First, an attack by white settlers, mistreatment by an Indian agent, or a treaty violation by the whites. Then Indian trouble. A small body of troops would be sent out to punish the Indians, and there would be casualties on both sides. This clash would be followed by outraged public demands that the Army be sent against the embittered tribes.

A completely new and decent Indian policy was imperative, the commissioners insisted.

Congress reluctantly appropriated funds to appease hostile tribes with gift of blankets, coffee, sugar, bacon, and flour. General Bill Harney was appointed superintendent of the northern Great Plains, with the authority to distribute almost a million dollars' worth of commodities among the tribes, according to his best judgment.

When he returned west to Nebraska, he was approached on a reservation near the North Platte by an elderly Indian woman who took him by the hand and shook it fervently.

"You did not know my father," she declared, "but he always said you were his friend. We trust no white man, Man-who-runs-like-the-Deer. But we trust *you!*"

Even now Congress was not motivated by justice for the Indian, but by the hope of winning cheap treaties that would let the transcontinental railroads penetrate the Indian hunting grounds and provide security for white settlers pushing west. During this pacification program, the settlers were busy filing legal claims to great tracts of public land in Kansas, Nebraska, and beyond. Pioneers who had once considered these lands too dry for farming now thought differently.

The Indians grew increasingly angry at this further betrayal of the treaties they had signed, agreeing to give up their lands in the east for territory in the west. Some tribes took to the warpath rather than parley any more with the Peace Commissioners when they returned west with the gifts Congress had voted to placate the Indians.

Once more the bugles blew, the colors and guidons fluttered in the wind, and the cavalry raised clouds of dust as they sought to subdue the embittered Indian nations. White pioneers of the west joined the campaign to "get rid of them pesky redskins." In many white settlements, Indians were shot on sight. Wherever gold was found, treaties were ignored.

When the Indian commissioners sought a new treaty with the Sioux, Chief Spotted Tail handed them an old treaty full of unfulfilled government promises. "No treaty," said Spotted Tail. "All men from Washington are liars."

In 1866, Ulysses S. Grant was appointed general of the Armies of the United States and sent an army after Sitting Bull. Secretary of War Edwin M. Stanton grew greatly upset and demanded to know by what authority Grant had taken it upon himself to start a new Indian war.

"I am not aware of any new war being waged against the Indians," Grant replied sardonically, "unless you mean the same one we have been fighting against them since the first white man set foot on the shores of America!"

But General Bill Harney doggedly refused to give up

hope that sooner or later his fellow countrymen would see the light and undergo a change of heart. Naïvely convinced—perhaps because he wanted to be—that Washington was at last ready to respect Indian treaties, he negotiated new ones with many Indian nations in 1867 and 1868.

The treaties set aside reservations for them and pledged the government to provide food, clothing, and other necessities; training in farming methods; farm equipment and seed; and schools for their children.

But even as the government invited the red man to "walk on the white man's road," the Supreme Court denied him American citizenship on grounds that since he was born into a tribal nation, he was not really born in the United States.

"If the original Americans are not citizens of the United States," Harney pointed out in testifying before Congress, "but are instead citizens of other nations, then how can our Government nullify the laws of those sovereign nations, as we always have done and continue to do? And why do we constantly repudiate our treaties with those nations as we would never dare do with the nations of Europe?"

No Congressman cared to answer those awkward questions.

But in 1869, General Sheridan proposed a cynical answer to President Ulysses S. Grant, who promptly accepted it. No more treaties would be made with Indian nations inasmuch as they were now "wards" of the government. As wards they could no longer deal as equals with their "trustee," but must depend upon Washington to protect, provide, and decide for them.

"The red man will wait for the Great White Father to

behave as father to the son," observed one Dakota chief, "as the field mouse waits to be fathered by the hawk."

Each passing year made it increasingly clear that the white man was determined to confine the Indians to reservation ghettoes to keep them from moving about freely to the west and being a "menace" to white development of the region. Not only was the government determined to sign no more treaties with the red man, but also to violate those it had already signed whenever this suited powerful white groups.

What happened in Michigan in 1869, as reported by the House Committee on Indian Affairs, was typical. Speculators in public lands discovered valuable minerals in part of a Chippewa reservation. The proper strings were pulled in Congress and those lands were promptly annexed by the government for public sale. But before the public was notified and had a chance to bid for them, speculators were allowed to grab them for a pittance, making a quick fortune.

Indian Commissioner Francis Walker (1871–73) spelled out the government's intentions toward its red wards with startling candor: "The Indians should be made as comfortable on, *and uncomfortable off*, their reservations as it was within the power of the Government to make them. . . . Such of them as went right should be protected and fed, and such as went wrong should be harassed and scourged without intermission."

Those who went "right" were, of course, the "good Injuns" who meekly submitted to confinement in the concentration camps where they had been herded. Those who went "wrong"—Apaches under Cochise, the Sioux under Crazy Horse and Sitting Bull, the Nez Perce under Chief

Joseph—constituted the "red devils" who demanded that the United States government honor its treaties with them.

By 1874, so many Indian nations were taking to the warpath that the American public, upset by these new outbreaks of hostility, was demanding to know what was wrong with the government's pacification program. In all fairness to the American people, it should be stated that they were consistently lied to by distorted reports in the press and did not really understand the Indian view.

This is not to imply that the motives of the reporters and press lords of the day were always sinister. Basically, their orientation was sensationalism—seizing upon any excuse for black headlines that would sell papers or magazines through the shock factor. It was this cheapjack journalism that made heroes of Billy the Kid, General Custer, Jesse James, Buffalo Bill, and other western celebrities.

The red man made a convenient scapegoat. Few white Americans thought to question why he was fighting so hard against the confiscation of his lands and the decimation of his peoples. Labeled a savage because he did not dress, eat, worship, live, or aspire as the white invaders of his country did, he was marked for extinction.

When the Indian nations refused to accept the white man's edict that they had no claim even to the western half of their own country, their armed risings sincerely baffled white Americans, who put pressure on Congress by their demand for an explanation. The House Committee on Indian Affairs felt compelled to hold a congressional investigation.

Summoned to testify as a key witness, a retired Army general who knew more about the Indians than any man of his time appeared before the House Committee on February 4, 1874.

The committee chairman asked General Bill Harney to name the Indian tribes with whom he had had experience.

"Principally with the Sioux and Cheyennes and all the Indians of the Plains and the Florida Indians," replied the seventy-four-year-old veteran. "I was very intimately acquainted with the Sioux for a great many years, and have been stationed among the Winnebagoes, Menomenees and other Indians."

The chairman asked him why he felt that he had done a better job of supervising their affairs than the Indian Bureau.

"The Indians have more respect for the military," he replied. "The Indians are robbed continually. That, I think, is pretty well-known, and I assert it positively. I know it of my own knowledge. That is the principal cause of Indian difficulties, I think. In fact, if we would keep our treaty stipulations with the Indians, we would have no trouble with them. The Indians do not violate their treaty stipulations, except when they are driven to it by the whites."

The chairman deliberated. "Do you think that it is the disposition of Indian tribes to observe treaty stipulations?"

"Yes. I have never known but two instances in which they violated treaties." He went on to elaborate the special reasons for those two nations, adding, "There was some excuse for them, but still they were punished."

"Are these Indian wars incited by the settlers, General Harney, or are they brought about by the Army?"

"It is principally the whiskey sellers and the Indian agents that make the difficulty. The Indian agents go out there to feather their own nests. Agents should never open a box or any other package till the Indians are all present to witness the operation. This would prevent any difficulty or trouble." He went on to insist that distribution of supplies to the Indians would be more honest under Army auspices, because "there cannot be stealing in the Army."

The chairman asked, "From your knowledge of the Indian character, do you believe that those people are to be controlled in any way except by fear of punishment?"

"Yes, sir," Harney replied promptly. "Kind treatment and *justice* can do it. They know what justice is, and they want it. If they are treated with justice, we will never have any trouble with them."

He was asked how he would prevent the introduction of whiskey among the Indians. He replied angrily, "I would hang the whiskey-sellers or shoot them. They are the very worst class of people on the frontier." Would he also hang the Indian agents who stole Indian goods? "Decidedly!"

These were strong views, and indefensible in the light of the constitutional guarantees of rights to trial of all accused persons. But they reflected the primitive notions of justice held by most frontiersmen of 1874. Certainly more cheats, horse thieves, and other undesirables of the west died at the end of a rope than were punished by the due process of law and order. It was significant that Harney, when pinned down, was not willing to trust vigilante justice.

"Would it be safe," he was asked, "to arm the settlers and let them take care of the frontier?" Trusting the Army but not the pioneers, he replied, "I do not think it would."

"As between fighting the Indians and giving them kind treatment, which would you say was the preferable course?"

"Kind treatment in the first place. If we comply with our treaty stipulations, we will have no difficulty at all."

"From the investigations that you made . . . did you come to the conclusion that the Indians were the wronged parties, and that the wars and troubles which had arisen with the Indians were caused by white men?"

"Decidedly so," Harney replied emphatically.

An outraged member of the House committee angrily demanded to know whether his observations were not based on the poor quality of Indian agents in the Indian Bureau twenty years earlier, rather than as of 1874.

"I do not think they were as corrupt then," he replied grimly, "as they are *now!*"

But the investigation changed nothing.

Totally disillusioned, General William Selby Harney retired to his home in St. Louis. He died shortly after his seventy-sixth birthday, perhaps the greatest unsung military hero in the history of the United States—at least by the standards of today's enlightened, socially aware generation.

News of his death sent many Indian nations, who remembered the one white man who had cherished and respected them, into mourning for the best friend and most esteemed enemy the American red man ever had.

In honor of his ascension to the Happy Hunting Grounds, the Sioux changed the name of Man-who-runs-like-the-Deer to one of greater significance.

His posthumous name—one of which he would have been deeply proud—was Man-who-always-kept-his-word.

The Hippies Go Indian

15

By 1882, the persistent injustice of the American government toward the red man led a group of Philadelphians to establish the Indian Rights Association. They worked for legislation and court decisions indemnifying tribes victimized by the cattle and mining interests, and by other white groups who had used the government to defraud Indians.

Five years later Congress was still passing anti-Indian legislation. In 1877, the Indian Allotment Act, introduced by Senator Henry L. Dawes of Massachusetts, finally brought to fruition the plan to split up tribal lands into individual family holdings, so that the land sharks could buy them up more easily. By 1927, Indian holdings of 140 million acres had dwindled to 50 millions, despite desperate pleas by Indian chiefs to their people not to sell to the white man.

"What!" the famous chief Tecumseh had exclaimed. "Sell land! As well sell air and water. The Great Spirit gave them in common to all." But tribal ties had been weakened through division of the land and encouragement of each family to make out on its own, in imitation of the white man.

"Offer this Indian and that one $3,000—it is more money than he ever heard of in his life, and he can imagine no end to it," observed the late Indian expert Oliver La Farge wryly. "If necessary, get him drunk. Talk him into signing a mortgage he cannot pay off, does not understand that he must pay off, and in due course foreclose. . . . That is the system."

By 1933, La Farge pointed out, 75 percent of Indian-owned lands had been lost to the red man's ownership by such means. Government policies had also accomplished the destruction of tribal society; the introduction of Indian children as domestic servants, farmers, and day laborers; and the denial of all avenues of protest to tribal spokesmen.

"All authority was taken away from the tribal leaders who refused to serve as puppets under the Army and the Indian Bureau," accused the nation's most honest United States Commissioner of Indian Affairs, John Collier. "To kill the Indian traditions and to break the relationship of the generations, Indian children were seized at six years and were confined in 'boarding schools' until past their adolescence. In vacation time they were indentured to whites as servants. . . . Everything reminiscent of or relevant to Indian life was excluded; the children were forced to join (Christian churches)."

An embarrassed government finally awarded the Indians American citizenship in 1924. But even then most Indians were kept from voting by restrictive state laws. It was not until ten years later, during the New Deal administration of President Franklin D. Roosevelt, that the government first showed genuine concern for the plight of the red man.

This concern was manifest in the appointment of Collier to head the Bureau of Indian Affairs. An outstanding world authority on Indians, Collier had spent almost all of his life, like Harney, in studying their culture and in fighting for their right to self-determination and self-government. It was Collier who inspired the Indian Reorganization Act of 1934, designed to establish Indian political and economic home rule; to protect the tribes against unscrupulous whites; and to provide them with better educational opportunities.

Collier stirred the nation's conscience, crying out, "Who can look on the condition of the Indians today—poverty-stricken, dying at twice the white man's rate of mortality, limited in education and opportunity, hopeless, distrustful —and not say that a reversal of Government policy is indicated?"

He praised the red man's culture as superior to that of the white man, declaring, "It is *we* who are poor—not the Navajo!" Instead of "civilizing" the Indian, he insisted, we should do everything possible to preserve and understand Indian art, music, folklore, and custom.

Collier proved to the Indians that he was sincere by replacing over half the employees in the Indian Bureau with Indians. He substituted day schools on the reservations, where Indian children were allowed to learn and talk in their own language, for boarding schools away from the tribes that had tried to brainwash them into becoming imitation white men.

Collier's reforms ended the allotment system; prohibited the unrestricted sales of Indian land; won tribal credit from federal funds; fostered tribal enterprises; and ended the use of force to compel tribal obedience to the government.

"It is merely a beginning," Collier insisted, "in the process of liberating and rejuvenating a subjugated and exploited race living in the midst of an aggressive civilization far ahead, materially speaking, of its own."

World War II brought further changes. Nearly seventy thousand Indian men and women from the reservations went into military service and the defense industries. This wider exposure to the world outside the reservations led Indians to demand more educational and job opportunities.

The government introduced a program of vocational training for Indians and sought to locate new industries on Indian reservations, to bring more Indians into the main currents of American life in the latter half of the twentieth century.

Another milestone in the government's effort to atone for the shameful treatment of the Indians was the Claims Commission Act of 1946. This commission was set up to hear tribal complaints of land fraud by the federal government. Of 917 claims filed by September 1967, 570 had been heard and 92 awards totaling some $241 millions had been made to the defrauded tribes. Most of these awards were earmarked for tribal community and economic development.

In 1953, a joint resolution of Congress led to a series of bills ending the "ward" status of Indians, making them—at long last—full-fledged American citizens with all the same rights and obligations as other citizens. Not all government officials, however, considered the timing of this resolution in the best interests of the red man.

"It would be incredible, even criminal," warned Secretary of the Interior Fred Seaton in 1958, "to send any Indian tribe out into the mainstream of American life until and unless the educational level of that tribe was one which was equal to the responsibilities which it was shouldering."

Oliver La Farge was inclined to agree: "It takes more than one generation to make the jump from a home in which no English is spoken, where the very sight of a white man is a rarity, where the thinking is the same as it was 300 years ago, to full competence in our alien and complex way of life."

When Stewart L. Udall became Secretary of the Interior under President John Kennedy in 1961, he appointed a task force to study Indian affairs. After a five-month field study, the task force recommended greater efforts to attract industries into locating plants on reservations; more vocational training and job placement; more credit to Indians who wanted to start small businesses on their own; more civil rights for Indians; speedier settlements by the Indian Claims Commission; and wider publicity to make white Americans understand the special problems of red Americans.

These objectives moved closer to realization with the appointment of Robert L. Bennett, an Oneida Indian, as Commissioner of Indian Affairs. He was sworn into office by the President on April 27, 1966.

"The time has come," Lyndon B. Johnson declared, "to put the first American first on our agenda . . . to begin work on the most comprehensive program for the advancement of the Indians that the Government of the United States has ever considered. I want it to be sound, realistic, progressive, venturesome and farsighted. . . . If you fulfill this charge, you will have the full power of the institution of the Presidency of the United States behind you."

Taking the President at his word, Bennett promptly called nine regional meetings at which he conferred with 153 tribes and intertribal groups, hearing almost 2,000 recommendations made by the Indians for bettering their condition. These recommendations, studied carefully by Secretary of the Interior Stewart Udall, led to the passage of the Indian Resources Development Act of 1967.

The Nation, a severe critic of the Johnson administration, nevertheless acknowledged that this act was "beyond doubt the most important single piece of Indian legislation to come before Congress in more than thirty years."

Basically, it made half a billion dollars in loans available to tribes to build up their own communities, making possible Indian-owned and operated businesses, civic improvements, modern schools, new housing units, and so forth.

Industry has also begun to cooperate. Over 94 companies now operate in Indian areas, with a combined Indian payroll of over $15 million annually. Tribes themselves have invested over $12 million of government credits, matched by $60 million of private investments, to help finance new industry in reservation areas. Among the companies who have built plants to train and utilize the skills of Indian labor are Fairchild Camera and Instrument Corporation and the Bulova Watch Company.

General Omar N. Bradley, now representing Bulova,

declares that the Chippewas working in their Turtle Mountain plant in North Dakota are "every bit as talented as the most skilled craftsmen producing jewel bearings abroad." Fairchild said of the Navajo, "They quickly learn the skills of transistor assembly and have a high productivity level."

But encouraging as these developments are, they only scratch the surface. The candid speech by President Johnson on March 6, 1968, made that fact abundantly clear.

Today only 600,000 Indians are left of the once proud Indian nations that inhabited all of America. Two-thirds still live on or near reservations as members of 784 tribes or bands. The largest reservations are in Arizona, New Mexico, and Oklahoma. Many of the older Indians still speak no English. Only 5,000 young Indians go further than a high school education. Fewer than 3,000 are enrolled in vocational schools. Only 1,300 get on-the-job training.

The vast majority of the Indian people go on living in the same wretched circumstances they have known ever since the American government penned them up in reservations.

American Indian artists in the entertainment world are doing all they can to aid their neglected people. Kay Starr, a successful singer who is part Choctaw, Cherokee, and Iroquois and was born on an Oklahoma reservation, is helping to raise $2 million for a Los Angeles Indian Center to serve that area's 45,000 impoverished Indians.

Folk singer Buffy Sainte-Marie, a Cree Indian maid from Saskatchewan, refused to star in a television episode of *The Virginian* until the producer first agreed to hire 37 real Indians to play all Indian parts and promised to have an anthropologist on hand to authenticate all artifacts, language, and customs of the Shoshone tribe being portrayed.

"There are thousands of Indians out of work," she explained. "Some of these are actors. . . . If an Indian can't play an Indian, he's had it, period. To get studios out of the easy habit of settling for non-Indian actors, I'm risking my chance to act." She went on to explain her insistence upon absolute authenticity in portraying the Shoshone:

"Ever since movie Westerns began, non-Indians have played Indians, and always badly. Therefore the Indian has consistently faced a world that takes us for carnival clowns, subjects for Halloween parties—either 'ignorant savages' or 'proud, noble heroes.' "

When the ABC-TV network planned to program a television series based on General George Custer's life and adventures, portraying the swashbuckling Indian-fighter as a great hero, the National Congress of Indians protested indignantly. Their protest was supported by an Episcopal bishop, Rt. Rev. W. W. Horstick of Eau Claire, Wisconsin, who insisted, "This series must not go on TV. It would cause irreparable damage to the image of Indians as human beings and as people trying to join the modern technological world. All the old hatreds would come to the surface." ABC-TV agreed and cancelled the series.

On the positive side, Tulsa, Oklahoma, staged a week-long cultural salute to its Indians in November 1967. A ceremonial Indian ballet by Cherokee composer Louis Ballard was presented with four famous part-Indian ballet dancers—Rosella Hightower, Marjorie Tallchief, Yvonne

Chouteau, and Moscelyne Larkin. Yvonne Chouteau said, "I became so emotionally involved in my variation about the 'Trail of Tears' that my husband was afraid I'd scalp the nearest white man!"

Rosella Hightower revealed that she had found an advantage to being Indian while traveling abroad recently as part of a French troupe touring Asia. In Red China there had been a bad moment when an examination of credentials revealed that she was an American. "Then I told them I was an Indian," she said, "and suddenly I was a victim of American society, a member of a downtrodden race—and treated better than anyone else!"

Ironically, the red man so long despised, scorned, and persecuted by generation after generation of white Americans became the object of a cult of veneration for some of the newest generation—the hippies of the late 1960's. Rejecting modern American society and culture as "second-rate" and "up-tight," many hippies dropped out to seek and adopt the ways and spiritual values of the original Americans.

Instead of white America's emphasis on rugged individualism and aggressive competition as a way of life, they hopefully sought a more loving, peaceful system in the Indians' tribal patterns of community living.

In Milbrook, New York, the hippies lived in tepees; in Santa Fe in hogans; in Big Sur in tents. Some went to the southwest to learn from the Pueblos and Hopis how to live off the land, find wild vegetables and herbs, raise corn and rabbits, weave baskets, stalk game, and tan hides.

They asked Indian tribal elders for guidance in setting

up their own communal societies, settling arguments by powwows, establishing group ceremonials and rituals. Even in the cities, many hippie groups sought to live according to tribal patterns, while adopting Indian dress like leather breachclouts, fringed squaw dresses, and Indian beads.

Hippies who broke the law by smoking marijuana claimed a psychedelic kinship with the Kikapoos and other tribes who practiced the Peyote Cult. This religious ceremony involved eating a spineless cactus button that produced trances accompanied by brilliant colors and psychedelic visions.

Hippies who pitched hogans near tribal reservations studied and practiced ceremonials of the red man like the Apache devil dance and the Navajo medicine dance. "Hippies," said Chief Rolling Thunder of the Shoshones, "are the reincarnation of the traditional Indians who have fallen. They are the ghosts of warriors who have come back to reclaim their lands."

But while many hippies sought to adopt the ancient ways of Indian life, most genuine Indians sought to escape the old ghetto life of the reservations to enjoy the very benefits of white America that the hippies were rejecting.

The North Dakota Indians not only joined the Poor People's March on Washington in the early summer of 1968, but then returned to the nation's capital afterward to press their demands upon a still-reluctant Congress.

"We need more money for our lands, better food, jobs, improved housing," insisted Rose Crow Flies High, a member of the governing body of three affiliated tribes of North Dakota. "And we'd like to decide things for ourselves!"

Tillie Walker, an Indian woman arrested and jailed during the Poor People's March, told Washington officials defiantly, "I challenge any bureaucrat to go and live on an Indian reservation. Try to overcome the oppression that has been ours for many, many years—for as long as the Bureau of Indian Affairs and the Department of Interior have been our brokers!"

Most white Americans were shocked in 1968 when the Koerner Commission appointed by President Johnson to study the treatment of non-white Americans in the United States reported its finding that our nation is a "racist society." Many white Americans, sobered by this judgment, are only now beginning to appreciate the injustices suffered under our government not just by the black man, but by the red man, too, since the beginning of our history on this continent.

Outbreaks of violence in the Negro slums of America made white Americans aware that giant steps had to be taken to bring the American dream to black as well as white citizens. Indians suffering in the slums of the reservations now wonder whether their own plight will continue to be ignored until they follow this example and take to the warpath.

"They know what justice is, and they want it," General Bill Harney warned America almost a century ago. But the Indians have never yet received more than a fraction of what is due them from the government that took away their lands and paid them in broken promises.

Some idealistic young Americans have organized indignant petitions to their Congressmen, insisting that the demands of Indians today be met. But the red man, desperately poor and underprivileged in the land where his fore-fathers once ruled supreme, still waits for an honest measure of justice at the hands of the white man.

One day, he hopes, the American government will finally keep faith with its great white general—the patriot it constantly betrayed, but who was enshrined in the hearts of the Sioux and all Indian nations as Man-who-always-kept-his-word.

Bibliography

(*Indicates Recommended Reading)

American Heritage, Editors of. *The American Heritage Pictorial History of the Presidents*. New York: American Heritage Publishing Co., Inc., 1968.

Berky, Andrew S., and James P. Shenton. *The Historians' History of the United States*. New York: G. P. Putnam's Sons, 1966.

*Collier, John. *Indians of the Americas*. New York and Toronto: New American Library, 1947.

Cooke, David C. *Fighting Indians of the West*. New York: Dodd, Mead & Company, 1954.

Custer, Elizabeth B. *Following the Guidon*. New York: Harper & Brothers, 1890.

Downey, Fairfax. *Indian-Fighting Army*. New York: Charles Scribner's Sons, 1941.

Flanagan, John, T. (ed.). *America Is West*. Minneapolis: University of Minnesota Press, 1945.

Holland, J. G. *Life of Abraham Lincoln*. New York: Paperback Library, Inc., 1961.

Johnston, Charles H. L. *Famous Scouts*. Boston: L. C. Page & Company, Publishers, 1910.

*La Farge, Oliver. *A Pictorial History of the American Indian*. New York: Crown Publishers, Inc., 1956.

Lowie, Robert H. *Indians of the Plains*. New York: McGraw-Hill Book Company, Inc., 1954.

MacFarlan, Allan A. *Living Like Indians*. New York: Association Press, 1961.

McKnight, Charles. *Our Western Border*. Philadelphia: J. C. McCurdy & Co., 1876.

Meriam, Lewis. *The Problem of Indian Administration*. Baltimore: Johns Hopkins Press, 1928.

Myers, Gustavus. *History of Great American Fortunes*. New York: Modern Library, 1937.

Reavis, L. U. *The Life and Military Services of General William Selby Harney*. St. Louis: Bryan, Brand & Co., Publishers, 1878.

Rister, Carl Coke. *Border Captives*. Norman: University of Oklahoma Press, 1940.

Schmeckebier, Lawrence F. *The Office of Indian Affairs*. Baltimore: Johns Hopkins Press, 1927.

*Tebbel, John, and Keith Jennison. *The American Indian Wars*. New York: Harper & Brothers, Publishers, 1960.

U.S. Department of the Interior (Bureau of Indian Affairs). *Commissioner of Indian Affairs. Annual Reports 1832–1865*. Washington: Government Printing Office, 1961.

Winther, Oscar Osburn. *The Old Oregon Country*. Bloomington: Indiana University Publications, 1950.

*Wisler, Clark. *Indians of the United States*. Garden City, N.Y.: Doubleday & Company, Inc., 1956.

Index